C000072057

DEBT-FREE LIVING IN 3 STEPS

HOW TO GET OUT AND STAY OUT OF CRUSHING
DEBT FAST WITH SIMPLE CHANGES YOU CAN
IMPLEMENT OVER THE NEXT 7 DAYS.

TERENCE THORNTON

CONTENTS

Untitled   5

Personal Finance Introduction   7

STEP 1: MONEY MINDSET

1. Debt: What is it, really?   17

2. Interest: The Devil's in the Details   36

3. Debt Psychology 101   50

STEP 2: GETTING YOUR DUCKS IN A ROW

4. Time to get friendly with your expenses!   67

5. The Master Plan: Let's Create It   81

6. Emergency Fund: Saving for the rainy day... or   95
   a few

STEP 3: CRUSHING DEBT FOREVER!

7. Envelope System: Back to Basics   109

8. It's Game Time!: Stick to the Plan   120

Conclusion   133

References   135

DEBT-FREE CHECKLIST

This checklist includes...

the three checkpoints needed to ensure you are on track to becoming debt-free, forever!

At the end of each month you will:

1. Go through the checklist.

2. Identify any of the checkpoints you are lacking in.

3. Make the appropriate changes for the following month until you are regularly checking off all boxes!

To receive your FREE checklist, scan the QR code or visit the URL below:

https://terence.activehosted.com/f/3

PERSONAL FINANCE INTRODUCTION

"You've got to tell your money what to do or it will leave."

— DAVE RAMSEY, AUTHOR AND
FINANCIAL ADVISOR

Have you found yourself in this position before? You work hard, you think that you are doing right by your money yet there never seems to be enough? Does your money just up and leave you? Take it from me. I truly understand what it means to look at your bank account and have that sinking feeling in the pit of your stomach. You may be looking at my credentials thinking, "what does this guy know about the pain of watching your hard-earned money flow right out of your pockets?" I can assure you that I have been in your shoes.

PERSONAL STRUGGLES

My name is Terence Thornton and I was once under the unbearable weight of more than $100k in student loan debt. Let me say that again. I was ONCE under the unbearable weight of more than $100k in student loan debt. I watched my bank account dwindle every month as money went out faster than I could earn it. I was stressed, terrified, and saw not even a sliver of light at the end of the tunnel. Until...

Until I got sick and tired of being sick and tired! Do you know what I mean? I was so tired of working and not being able to go out to see a movie, hang out with my friends at the bar or even grab a coffee with a friend in fear that my debit card would be declined and my pockets empty. I hated the fact that I watched my checking account and my spending like a hawk and yet I still could not make ends meet.

I was working a 9 to 5 job, earning approximately $46k per year, which should have been sufficient for a twenty-something to live on and to live well. I was single, had no children, and yet I was living paycheck to paycheck, terrified whether I could actually make next month's rent. Why did I have to live this way? I was horrified at the thought of living my entire life like this.

My parents had taught me the value of savings, the concepts of good and bad debt, and the theory behind credit and credit cards. I thought I knew what I was doing but like you, I was still burdened by this thought that my future was doomed to living on a shoestring budget! If I was this stressed about my finances in my twenties with no family yet, what was I going to do once I did get married and possibly have children? How was I going to pay off the enormous amount of debt that I had incurred in college, pay for everyday living expenses of a family, AND plan for the future? No one had prepared me for how difficult this journey of adulthood and money was going to be.

As activist Fannie Lou Hamer is so famously quoted as saying, I was "sick and tired of being sick and tired." Granted, my financial woes seem trivial in comparison to her struggles for equality. However, the saying very appropriately defines my feelings about my finances just five short years ago. I was already sick of the financial hardship that I was experiencing, and life had not even yet gotten really hard. I was determined to put a stop to the stress that I was feeling, and I knew that the only way that I was going to be free from under the burden was to take control. As Dave Ramsey says, I had to tell MY money what to do!

TAKING CONTROL

I was intrigued by this idea that I could control my finances rather than my finances controlling me. Have you ever thought about this concept of controlling your finances? Probably not. Most people work, pay their bills, maybe save a little for a rainy day, and spend what is left. What if you decided to think about your money differently and try to control the what, how, and more importantly, WHY your money has been leaving you and how you can make it stay? WOW! What a concept!! You have control over where your money goes and what you spend it on? This may certainly be a new concept for many of you.

I want to pull back the covers, throw open the blinds, and shed light onto many of the secrets that I have learned in the last 5 years. Once I got sick and tired of my finances controlling me and my life, and I decided to take back control, I got serious. I was NOT going to struggle to pay off my student loan; I was NOT going to live paycheck to paycheck; I was NOT going to look at my future and feel desperate and alone about my financial situation.

No! Instead, I WAS going to learn everything that I could about managing my finances. I WAS going to create a nest egg for my future, and I WAS going to create a legacy for my children that they knew came from hard work and by educating myself.

I made it my mission to study personal money management. I became passionate about finances and investing, and I got excited about my finances. In fact, after having paid off more than $100k in student loan debt, I got so excited that I decided that I just had to share this information with others who also may be struggling. I wanted to tell others who are in the same position that you are not alone. I've been in your shoes. I've done the work. I've declined the offers to go out for fear of anyone knowing how bad my finances were. I had tried everything that I knew how to do.

Once I made my mind up, there was no stopping me! I was like a freight train heading full steam ahead. What I learned along my journey helped me to pay off that $100k in student loan debt and I now dedicate myself as a Personal Finance Writer to sharing this information with others. Helping people get control of their debt and finances brings me great joy because I know that if I could do it, you can too!

I was able to relieve myself of the pain, embarrassment, and anxiety that my finances caused me. I can now live my life how I want. I can imagine the future that I want for my children and I even have envisioned how I will live my life in retirement. Does that sound too far off to even think about? Well, how do you think most people can retire? Did they wake up one day and say, "today is the day that I am going to retire?" Well, there might be some people out there who can do that, but the majority of retirees in the world have been financially planning for their retirement for their entire working life.

TAKE THE BULL BY THE HORNS

Remember that I was in your shoes. I took the bull by the horns and changed my life by changing my finances. I am so passionate about this topic that I just had to share it with you. I feel that this information is so important that it would be wrong of me to keep it to myself. Why wouldn't I want everyone to have the financial freedom that I have experienced? Helping you to achieve control over your debt and personal finances will further validate that my system, my solution to debt management, truly works. You may even find that you were already doing some of the things that I will suggest to you just without the commitment and excitement that I will demonstrate to you.

Throughout this book, I am going to walk you through exactly how I was able to get out from under the weight of my student loan debt and live the life that I want, because I am passionate about it. I want you to feel the same excitement, relief, and happiness that I feel knowing the huge accomplishment I have reached. I am confident that you will feel the same way once you read and follow all of my suggestions in the following chapters.

Disclaimer: It is important to understand that changing your finances and putting more money in your bank account is NOT going to happen overnight. The first step will be to change your outlook and relationship with money and the rest will flow from there. Although it took me five years to reach the point where I am now, your own journey may be quicker or slower depending on your amount of debt and your commitment to following the process. Trust me, though, when I tell you that I believe in you. If I can do it, you are fully capable of telling your money what to do, getting out from under the burden of debt, and living the life that you want.

When you are finished reading this book, it is my sincerest hope that you have been inspired, motivated, educated, and are well on your way to financial freedom. I expect that you will have gained a sound understanding of many of the following concepts:

- · What debt is
- · The theory behind interest
- · The psychology behind debt
- · How to get control of your expenses
- · How to make changes to your spending
- · Saving for a rainy day
- · The envelope system
- · Sticking to the plan

Now you know that there are about a million other people out there who tout that they are the expert in personal finance, and maybe in fact they are. What makes me different? Why should you listen to me over any of the other financial gurus in the industry? I am not suggesting that you should NOT read any of the material published by some of the greats in financial management. No. In fact, you SHOULD read their material and heed their advice. That is how I learned. I soaked in every bit of information that I could find about debt management, saving, and retirement, and then I tailored it to what fit best for ME.

But I did more than simply learn. I used the knowledge that these so-called experts put out in their books, webinars, seminars, and courses and I added a very special ingredient! Passion! My passion for not only the subject of personal finance, but bigger still, to get myself out of debt is what has fueled how I intend to deliver this information to you.

Will you gain a lot of insight from those other advisors and professionals? Of course! There is no disputing that they will give you profound insight into the world of personal finances. But what I intend to give you is the will and desire to take the bull by the horns to not only make a change but to be committed to achieving the results that you want.

That is the reason that you have picked up this book, right? You want to see a difference in your bank account, and you are sick and tired of the struggle. Because you have picked up a book and not just any book, you have picked up THIS book, I can already tell that you have a deeper connection with your debt and your finances than most people, and you are passionate like I was about telling your money what to do!!

So, what are you waiting for? Let's get started.

STEP 1: MONEY MINDSET

1

DEBT: WHAT IS IT, REALLY?

T here is a German Proverb that says, "He who is quick to borrow is slow to pay." I feel that this quote very accurately reflects that mindset and, unfortunately, the habits of most Americans. We find ourselves in a pinch or in a "want" position and our gut reaction is to borrow the money from creditors, banks, and even family or friends.

WANTS VERSUS NEEDS

For most of us, borrowing to pay for large purchases such as college education or a home is a part of life, but what about those trips to the mall or the car you need to get to work? Older generations did not utilize this concept of debt in the way that we do today. If they were looking to buy a car, they saved up the money first and then made the purchase. In our society of instant gratification, we are all the more ready to buy it now and pay for it later.

Although this concept of debt and borrowing money is as old as time, it is our relationship to money and things now that causes many people to fall into the debt trap. I will get into this in a minute. I want to just take you back through time to look at the origins of debt and credit, although I won't bore you with too many details.

Long before societies used money as a means of transacting, ancient peoples used the barter system or borrowing to get what they needed. A perceived value was placed on the goods or service and it was 'collected' in the form of reciprocity and relied on mutual trust. People could in essence "run a tab" and make "payments" when and as they could. As civilizations grew and expanded, coins began to be used to assign economic value to goods and services. Citizens had to have a means of "earning" coins in order to be able to pay the newly imposed taxes plus interest as it accrued. For those who could not pay, they were forced into slavery as a means to pay off their debt.

EXTENSION OF CREDIT

During the middle ages, paper money and promissory notes emerged. As empires were formed, capitalism and more importantly, the acquisition of riches began to prevail. Military armies were funded through the extension of credit with the expectation that with the spoils of war and the conquering of nations, the debt would be repaid.

Capitalism itself was created on this idea of the extension of credit as individuals and businesses strive to earn a profit and borrow against their future earnings. Through this economic system, countries have risen from the throes of poverty, homelessness and famine, to industrial and technologically advanced nations in which the distribution of wealth is grossly unequal and people bury themselves under mounds of debt.

According to the Merriam-Webster Dictionary, debt is defined as a "state of being under obligation to pay or repay someone or something in return for something received." This definition does not sound very far off from where the idea began many centuries ago, right? In other words, you received a good or service in advance of paying for it and now you must pay it back. This concept would not be so bad if repayment were not based on various conditions revolving around repayment and specifically, the amount required to pay for the use of the money in advance.

Debt is in simple terms deferred payment. I am sure that you have seen and possibly even taken advantage of those offers for furniture or appliances advertising--buy now pay later. The idea is that you can reap the benefit of the item you are purchasing and not technically have to pay for it until the end of the term, for example, 12 or 24 months from the date of purchase. Sounds great, right? For most consumers this is an easy way of satisfying their need for instant gratification and having an extended period to pay for it. In theory, it works well IF the note is repaid within the time period specified. If not, then the creditor is entitled to receive a very large amount of money in return for them allowing you to use that product.

This is where many people get stuck. Remember the original quote I used? "Quick to borrow and slow to pay"? Consumers think it is a good idea to buy something and pay for it in small increments later, but then life happens and they do not end up paying for it as required until it is too late and they are hit with the high interest and fees. Now, instead of having paid $1799 for the new refrigerator, they may end up paying $2250 or more once the debt is paid including finance charges. Their attempt to defer payment has now cost them a lot of money with no added value. In other words, their refrigerator did not become more valuable over time and in fact, the opposite is true. Goods lose value as they age and so they have paid more for an item that is no longer worth even what they originally intended to pay for it.

DAWN OF A NEW AGE

Until the 1950s, revolving credit lines were opened at banks and through merchants by which consumers could use credit to purchase goods. To keep track of these transactions, merchants began using an imprinted card or coin. As capitalism expanded and consumers could now shop at multiple merchants, a new system was devised to keep track of many transactions on one line of credit and thus, the emergence of the credit card.

For its short history of less than 75 years, the concept of credit card has certainly put people on the fast track to financial difficulties and overwhelming debt. As of Q3 2019, consumer debt in the U.S. crossed the $1 trillion mark. Millions of Americans, 189 million to be exact, carry credit card debt, and on average have four or more credit cards in their name.

The concept of debt itself and creditors has grown to the tune of $13.86 trillion of consumer debt, according to the New York Federal Reserve as of mid-year 2019[1], including mortgages, car payments, credit cards and student loans each of which I will talk about in more detail.

MISMANAGEMENT OF MONEY

So, we know the history of debt and we touched a little bit about credit cards, but I want to dive in a bit deeper about the psychology of debt that I alluded to earlier. Credit itself and the borrowing of money is not as evil as some people may think. Unfortunately, it is the mismanagement of it that is the problem that millions of people find themselves in.

Credit used to be a means to ensure that consumers could purchase their basic needs such as food, seed, and supplies while having a little extra time to pay for them. In recent years, the credit card has become an extension of a person's hand; a means of meeting a need instantly yet deferring payment for some people as long as they want.

There are many people who use the credit card simply as a means of payment--instead of carrying around cash to pay for everything from coffee to gas and groceries. For others, the credit card allows them to make unnecessary, extravagant or outlandish purchases that they may never be able to pay off.

It is a person's relationship to money and spending which determines whether they develop healthy or unhealthy spending habits and, therefore, the resulting debt is incurred. I want to touch on spending behaviors only briefly here. I will dive into this subject deeper in Chapter 3, not only about habits but more importantly, the mindset of money, debt, and how to live debt-free.

HEALTHY BEHAVIOR

People who have a healthy relationship and perception of their finances often do a reality check of their financial situation. They evaluate the risks involved in spending in excess of their budget and are aware of the reality of having the funds to pay back the amount borrowed through a loan or via a credit card in a reasonable amount of time. They understand the value of credit to help them make large purchases such as a home or for college education, and they see the potential return on investment. People with a healthy perspective understand the additional responsibility that debt brings on and make it their priority to pay off the loans as quickly as possible.

A person with this type of perspective on their money may use a credit card to pay for everyday purchases yet has the means of paying off the credit card at the end of each month, therefore not incurring any debt. On the other hand, another person may use a credit card for the same reason yet not have the physical means of paying the balance in full--and so we have debt!! For some people, using a credit card may be the only way that they can provide basic needs for their family at the moment, but unfortunately at a very high cost to their financial future.

UNHEALTHY BEHAVIOR

Before consumers had the luxury of using a credit card to make large purchases, they had to carefully consider their financial health and deliberately save enough money to make a purchase of a house, a car, a trip. They had to be certain that they could afford to pay for the good or service and for most people, it was a make or break decision.

Credit cards have made those decisions easier, with most people having to put little thought into the decision. They swipe away, buying sometimes recklessly to satisfy the instant need for gratification. They no longer have to wait until their next pay day or until they have squirreled away enough money to pay for it. Credit cards have taken away the need for consumers to be patient or persistent in their savings and spending habits. Spending becomes easier when a consumer swipes away not considering the amount that is being spent until in some cases, it is too late. This is completely opposite from using cash to make purchases. When you have no more cash in your hand, you simply can't buy anything else.

The extension of credit by creditors also feeds into a person's lack of willpower. Although instant gratification may not necessarily be a bad characteristic trait to have, it can be detrimental when combined with a person's inability to stop spending or feeding their need to buy. For many people, shopping fills a void and makes them feel good. Having the ability to simply whip out a credit card encourages them to keep on buying. If you went to the mall with $100 in your pocket and you knew that you only had $100 to spend, you would more than likely consider your purchases more carefully as well as display better control over your emotions and desire to feed the need.

Credit cards allow people to spend money they have not yet actually earned, putting them in a deficit financial position even before they set foot at work that week. Unfortunately, without a health perspective on money and debt, many consumers spend too freely and find themselves constantly in denial of their true financial situation.

Unfortunately, the abuse of credit cards can lead some people into much more serious problems. As interest accumulates each month, the debt becomes overwhelming and unmanageable, adding more stress to a possibly already stressful financial situation. As a result of unhealthy spending habits, people ultimately pay much more than intended for their purchases (with interest over time) and can cause severe damage to their ability to obtain credit for large purchases in the future.

When used responsibly, lines of credit and credit cards are a great way for people to reach their goals of owning a home, completing their education, or starting a business. However, if used irresponsibly they can lead to financial hardship, emotional and mental strain, and increased pressure.

Now that we have looked at the psychology of debt a little, and why and how debt can accrue, let's take a more detailed look at what debt is with the goal of understanding how it impacts your life. I am going to get a bit technical here, but I will be sure to give you definitions of some of the things I am talking about. It is important to understand the basics if you are to manage your financial situation such that you avoid debt, or if you have already incurred it, you can successfully get out of it.

TYPES OF DEBT

As I am sure you know, debt is in its simplest terms money that is owed by one party to another. However, there are several types of debt, each with its own benefits and disadvantages.

Unsecured debt versus secured debt

If you open your wallet and see a plastic card, you are probably familiar with unsecured debt. Credit cards are the most common and most expensive type of unsecured debt and the majority of American consumers have them.

Unsecured debt is not backed by an asset. In other words, the borrower is not required to guarantee repayment by attaching it to an already existing asset as collateral. Interest is charged on the outstanding balance to ensure that the creditor is compensated for the risk of extending credit to the borrower. The balance due will increase each month depending on the rate of interest or APR that the creditor has assigned to the account. I will talk about APR and interest in much more detail in the next chapter. Credit cards typically carry a maximum spending limit that is determined by a borrower's credit history and credit worthiness.

If a borrower defaults on payment (does not pay back the amount due), it may be difficult for the lender to recover the funds that they extended and, therefore, credit cards typically carry a higher interest rate to account for this risk. Credit card debt is considered to be the amount of money due to a credit card issuer or funder that is carried over as unpaid from month to month.

Secured debt is slightly different from unsecured debt in that repayment is guaranteed by a physical item which is used as collateral against the loan. In other words, if you as the consumer do not pay back the loan as agreed upon, the creditor has the right to seize the property as payment against the amount due. For example, you ask a bank to extend credit to you so that you can purchase a home. If you are unable to repay the loan monthly as established with the lender, they have every right to take back their property (i.e. foreclosure).

Consumer Debt

There are several different kinds of consumer debt and it is important to understand the differences between each one and how each can be used (or abused).

We have already talked about credit card debt fairly extensively. Hopefully you have a clear picture about what it is and how easily its use can get out of control quickly, creating a downward spiral in your financial situation if not managed properly. I'll address it in more detail in the next chapter when we talk about interest.

Personal loans are consistent with the more traditional method of borrowing money. Before the insurgence of credit cards, a merchant would extend credit to a consumer with an agreement that payments would be made to pay off the amount due. In my mind's eye, I envision a farmer making a deal with the local supply store in town for a line of credit or in other words, a personal loan that the farmer would repay as his crops began to produce and he could earn a profit.

Although most of us do not have to approach a store to obtain what we need to survive in this way, personal loans are now used to obtain a significant amount of cash for large purchases such as home remodeling, to consolidate credit card debt (at a lower interest rate), to plan a wedding, or to create an emergency fund. The terms of the loan usually require payment to be made over longer periods of time, like three to five years, and can be secured or unsecured. Of course, secured loans will have a lower interest rate and possibly higher borrowing limits. Unsecured personal loans will have more restrictions on what the funds can be used for.

Auto loans are a means by which those in need of a car can purchase a vehicle with the vehicle itself being used as the guarantee for repayment. They are typically long-term loans with the monthly payments relative to the value of the car. In other words, the more expensive the car that you want to drive, the higher your monthly payments will be.

A mortgage is a secured loan for the purchase of a primary residence or rental property. According to Forbes.com, nearly 40% of homes in the United States are free and clear of a mortgage. So, let's flip that number on its head: more than 60% of Americans pay the bank to live in their homes. Owning a home is typically the single biggest decision that many people will make in their personal finances during their lifetime, and it is not one that should be taken lightly. In 2017, the average American carried a mortgage balance of approximately $175k--that is certainly no small dollar amount owed to a lender.

With the changes in healthcare policy and the high cost of medical care, unfortunately, many consumers find themselves in debt to healthcare providers. Medical debt has been for years the number one reason that people file bankruptcy, which I will address in a minute. A routine visit to the doctor or a medical emergency could force many people into an unexpected financial position. Although providers do not usually charge interest, the cost of service alone may be more than a budget can bear.

Lastly, in order to fulfill our dreams and to achieve success in our careers, many of us rely on Federal or private student loans to pay for our continuing education. I say US because as I explained to you earlier, I came out of college with a staggering amount of student loans and the overwhelming burden of how I was going to pay for them. According to a recent study[2], most students begin their careers with an average of $37k in loans due to financial institutions. Depending upon your career choice, this may be more than your expected annual salary. With the rising costs of tuition and room and board, this figure is expected to increase in coming years.

Default on loans

Now you know that as a consumer, you are required to pay back the money that you borrow no matter what form of debt that you have incurred. The question is, what happens if you don't? If you are one of those people who pays off your credit card at the end of every month, kudos to you! You are probably not going to get much out of this book moving forward. This tells me that you have a pretty good handle on your finances and more than likely do not live outside your means.

You could still have other types of debt, though, which could be in jeopardy. There are consequences to not making regular payments on any type of consumer debt. If you do not pay, it is called defaulting on your debt.

Credit cards

If you have a balance due on your credit card and miss one payment, the lender will typically send you a friendly reminder with no additional consequence.

In the second month of a missed payment, you will receive a phone call about your past due account.

After three months, it is up to the credit card company to determine if they are going to send your account to collections or not.

Let's pause here for a second and take a look at what this means. A collection agency purchases a debt from the original creditor usually for a fraction of the amount owed. The debt is still due, but simply not to the original credit card company or lender. You will begin receiving notices from the collection agency regarding the next steps, which could include lawsuits, wage garnishment, a bank levy, or a lien on your property. Collections does not apply to credit cards alone. If you default on any of your debt accounts, the credit has the right to take action against you.

Auto loan

If you do not make your payment to the creditor for your car, you can rest assured that after contacting you to discuss your payment options, the bank will eventually send a tow truck to confiscate their property. Remember as we talked about earlier, auto loans are secured debt using the vehicle itself as collateral. If you think about it, your car is technically the property of the bank until you have fully paid off the debt at which time ownership transfers to you. No payments, no car!!!

Mortgage

Having a roof over your head is considered to be a necessity, but you still have to pay for it. If you default on your mortgage, the bank can seize your home and evict you from the property.

After a specific number of missed mortgage payments, the lender will send you a letter of foreclosure. They want you to catch up on your missed payments and avoid the foreclosure process, which is an expensive and lengthy process. Most lenders are open to negotiating payments with you based on your financial situation.

Rather than ignoring the calls and letters for payment, it is best that you are forthcoming and understand your options. Although foreclosure may be inevitable, it is important that you understand the consequences of not paying the debt owed on your mortgage.

Student loans

Since student loans can be obtained from several sources, the process and consequences if you default on your loan may be different for each.

Federal loans are considered delinquent after your first day of non-payment. In other words, miss your due date by one day, and your status moves from current to delinquent where it will remain for the next 90 days.

After 270 days, your loan is considered to be in default, and negotiations with the lender will no longer be possible. Instead, the entire amount owed will be due in full.

Since this type of loan is payable to the government, they are not likely to let you have a pass on a defaulted student loan but rather will take their money any way they can, including wage garnishment. They are legally entitled to put a lien on your home or garnish your income tax return for any outstanding balance. They could even sue for repayment--the government is serious about repayment of Federal student loans, so it is in your best interest to stay on top of payments.

Private lenders are even less tolerant of overdue student loan payments. After just one or two missed payments, your account may be considered in default and could be sent to collections.

Although they are limited in the actions that they can take against you, no lien or seizure of your property, they can take you to court for full payment of the outstanding balance. This process can be messy, expensive and time consuming.

I have talked about some of the consequences of defaulting on your consumer debt. While non-payment can leave you without a car, homeless, and owing more than you originally even borrowed, another serious impact that it has is on your credit score.

A credit score is a number that is assigned to a person that indicates their ability to repay a loan. Several factors contribute to the credit score assigned to you as a borrower, including your payment history, the amount owed, length of credit history, and outstanding balance against credit limits. Credit scores are reported to and monitored by credit reporting agencies such as Experian, TransUnion, and Equifax.

When you want to borrow money, lenders first check your credit score to determine your creditworthiness. In other words, your spending habits and diligence with repaying what you have previously borrowed. Although your history does not always dictate your future, creditors are interested in the trends that they see. When you make regular, on-time payments to creditors, they report positively to the reporting agencies. On the flip side, when you are late, delinquent, or in default on any type of debt, they report that as well.

Your credit score determines your ability to qualify for additional loans in the future. Lenders see defaults and late payments as higher risk and may either deny you credit for a loan, mortgage or credit card, or charge higher interest and fees to account for the higher risk. A poor credit score can follow you for up to seven years!! That is a significant length of time when it comes to your money, so be sure to manage your finances in such a way as to avoid any risk of damage to your score.

Obviously, that is easier said than done. But if you picked up this book and have read this far, you are in the right mindset and are eager to learn how to protect your credit reputation and financial health.

We have talked about a very wide range of topics in this chapter so let's do a little recap.

SUMMARY - DEBT: WHAT IS IT, REALLY?

- People have borrowed money to pay for goods and services for centuries.
- If you have debt, you are not alone.
- There are healthy and unhealthy spending behaviors that can lead to debt.
- Consumer debt comes in various forms.
- There are consequences to non-payment of your debt.

I have shared with you a little about me and the situation which led me to write this book. I had more than $100k in student loan debt that I had to get under control to avoid defaulting on, which I know could have caused a negative snowball effect on my financial situation and future. I followed the principles that I will outline in the next chapters to help me to avoid facing delinquency, negatively impacting my credit score, and hampering my ability to have control over my money. I could have easily slipped into a default situation had I not gotten a grip on my money. As Dave Ramsey says, "You've got to tell your money what to do or it will leave." I had to tell my money what to do to avoid paying unnecessary fees, higher interest, and expensive litigation.

I am so excited to share my story with you and these steps so that you can successfully keep hold of your money and live debt-free as well. My debt situation involved student loans, but these steps will help you to get a handle on your money no matter the type or combination of debt that you have incurred.

Keep reading "Debt-Free Living in 3 Steps" to continue to be inspired and motivated to achieve your own financial freedom.

2

INTEREST: THE DEVIL'S IN THE DETAILS

You have most certainly heard the phrase "the devil is in the details." But did you ever stop to think what it means? In other words, something might seem simple at first but is more complicated than you thought once you look at it closer. Unfortunately, this concept of interest falls into this category. It may seem very basic until you dive into it and understand how it impacts you and your finances. Possibly like you, at first glance, I thought that interest was fairly straightforward. I was very wrong.

WHAT IS INTEREST?

Interest is the fees earned and paid when a transaction is made to lend or borrow money and is calculated by an interest rate. In simple terms, it is additional money that you must pay to the lender for the privilege of using their money. They are taking a risk on you and are limited as to the use of their money, so they certainly want to be compensated for this inconvenience. However, do not be mistaken. This "inconvenience" of risk and limited use has become one of the largest industries in the country.

When you are considering borrowing money, no matter the mechanism (i.e. credit card, home mortgage, personal loan), the amount that you pay in interest will be dependent upon the value that you get in return. So, let's be clear. At some point, everyone will more than likely borrow money for something in their life. Maybe you want to buy a house. Is it worth it to you to pay the bank an additional amount of money for the privilege of living in your home? The bank is taking a risk on you; can you afford to pay the monthly mortgage? Do you have a steady income? What is your financial history like? They will be possibly lending you hundreds of thousands of dollars. They certainly want something in return for their belief in you that you will in good faith pay it back. Well, good faith doesn't have much to do with lending these days. During the time when a shop owner extended credit to a farmer to buy seed, it was in "good faith" that the farmer was obliged to pay it back plus interest. Now, you are obligated by law to pay back all that you have borrowed, including the interest that has accrued.

When considering borrowing money, there are several very important factors to take into consideration:

1. How much you want to borrow
2. The interest rate
3. How long it will take you to repay the loan

Now, just as I mentioned in the beginning of this chapter, the devil IS in the details. In the next few paragraphs, I am going to get a bit technical here. I put this out here not to scare you away or overwhelm you with facts and figures. No! It is important to understand exactly how this interest thing works so that you can make informed decisions about borrowing and debt. Remember the key to interest is that you are not only borrowing a sum of money from a lender but you are also PAYING to use it, so obviously you have to take this cost into consideration. This is where the details can get a little scary and where in fact, many people get consumed by debt because they did not fully understand the details.

TYPES OF INTEREST

So, let's get started by first understanding the various types of interest.

Fixed Interest

A fixed interest rate is the simplest and most common type of interest. It is very easy to calculate and is very stable.

Example: You borrow $1000 from the bank to make a purchase. The bank charges you a 5% interest rate for the use of their money. In return, you will repay the bank $1,050.00 over the term of the loan. So, if you promised to repay the bank within one year, your payments will be $87.50 per month.

Is it worth it for you to pay the additional $50 for the privilege of buying whatever it is you wanted?

Variable Interest

Unlike a fixed interest rate which does not change, a variable interest may change with the market. Lenders tie the prime interest rate that they offer to the base rate established by the Federal Reserve. As the market fluctuates and rates change, the interest owed by a borrower may also change.

Example: Let's look at that same $1000 loan that you take out to buy furniture. If the bank offers a variable rate of prime plus 3%, then as the prime rate changes, so will the amount that you owe. If the prime rate is 4%, then your loan carries a rate of 7%. The prime rate may vary during the term of your loan so the amount that you ultimately pay to the bank is also subject to change. Ultimately, you may repay the bank more than you bargained for.

Annual Percentage Rate (APR)

The APR is the amount of your total interest paid annually on the loan and is very popular with credit card companies. When you carry a balance from one month to the next on your credit card statement, the lender charges a rate that is usually prime plus a margin as decided by the bank. This margin is determined in part by how comfortable the bank is in your ability to repay the debt. Unfortunately, the less confidence that the lender has in you, the higher the margin that they are likely to charge.

Example: You apply for and are approved for a credit card with ABC Bank and because of several missed payments with a previous lender, the bank believes that there is a high risk that you may not be able to repay the loan that they have extended to you. So, they charge you a significant margin on the prime rate of 3.25% at 14.99% for an APR of 18.24% which is then used to calculate the amount of interest that will be applied to the balance.

On a $1000 balance, you can be confident that you will be charged $18.24 in interest for that month. Of course, the danger with this type of interest is that if you are only making small payments on the debt, the interest may be accumulating faster than you are paying it down. We will talk about this in more detail a bit later but for the moment it is safe to say that this is a dangerous place to be in.

Simple Interest

Simple interest is well, simple. It is the method that is most often used to calculate the amount of interest due from a borrower for a car or personal loan. It is beneficial for those people who generally pay their loans early or on-time since the interest is dependent in many cases upon the number of days between payments. Payment is first applied to the interest due for the period and the balance is paid toward the principal balance.

Example: You take out a car loan with a principal balance of $15,000 and a 5% simple interest rate. If your payment is due on July 1st and you make the payment on the due date, the lender will calculate the interest due based on 30 days in the previous month.

= $15000 x .05 = $750/year or $2.055/day x 30 days = $61.64

However, if you make payment on the loan on the 25th of the month, you will actually be saving on the interest charge.

= $2.055/day x 25 days = $51.38

In this scenario, more of your hard-earned money will be applied toward the principal versus paying the interest charges.

Compound Interest

While simple interest is just that, simple, compound interest is a bit more complicated. Interest compounds or is added to the principal or balance due making paying down this type of loan more difficult over time. Compounding interest is certainly beneficial when you are the lender of funds as the interest continually accrues on the balance. However, credit cards and student loans typically use compound interest to calculate the balance due.

Example: You take out a student loan in the amount of $10,000 at a compound interest rate of 10% for a term of three years. The amount of interest that will be paid by the end of the term will be $1,616.00 with a monthly payment of $323.00. The process of amortization is used with this type of loan to account for the reduction in principal and interest payments each month. Of course, the more that you pay each month which can be applied to the principal, the faster the loan will be repaid.

Prime Rate

Prime rate is a short-term interest rate that lending institutions use as the foundation of their own loan products. It is a convenient and consistent way for banks to offer competitive rates to clients to keep the economy moving. I discussed this earlier when I talked about variable rates, since many banks will add a margin to the prime rate to account for their use or borrowing of the funds. Banks often give the prime rate to "favored" customers with excellent credit scores for loans.

Example: You apply for a personal loan at a bank where you already have an established relationship, you have an excellent credit score and have proven your credit worthiness. The bank offers you a prime rate on the loan which is currently 3.25%.

Discount Rate

Reserved typically for financial institutions, a discount rate is a very low interest rate charged to cover lending of short-term funds, even for just one day. While it is not generally offered to the public, banks may take advantage of a discount rate to borrow money from another bank or the Federal Reserve to account for a daily shortage, a short-term crisis, or to correct liquidity.

As you can see from the many different types of interest rates, there can also be many pitfalls when it comes to borrowing money. Unfortunately, because many people do not fully understand how interest impacts their money and their ability to repay any balance borrowed, they can easily fall into the trap of debt and its overwhelming burden.

DANGERS OF DEBT

As we have been talking about, and the premise and motivation behind this book, there are obvious dangers to having debt. First off, having debt of any kind hanging over your head adds pressure to your finances.

It is certainly a common theory among the younger generations that "a little debt won't hurt you." Unlike the older generations as mentioned who saved for big purchases and only accepted the extension of credit when they were in dire need, many people are quick to swipe the credit card or take out that loan without doing a deep dive into how it will impact their life in the future.

If you have picked up this book, then you very well may be one of those people who has not given debt and its repercussions much thought . . . until now! Do not get me wrong. This is a no judgment zone! Remember I was in your shoes just a few short years ago. My point is simply that you are in this position and my goal is to help you get out of it.

First things first though is that we have to identify HOW you got into this position at all. In other words, the dangers of debt and where people easily are sucked into the convenience of the credit card world we live in. If you do not understand how you got here, or solve the root of the problem, you may find yourself in this same position again at some time.

Credit cards have become a way of life for most of us. We pull out the card at the mall, when we see that tempting vacation advertised on the television, and we even offer to pay for dinner for the entire table! Unfortunately for many people, when the end of the month rolls around and that statement arrives, they have forgotten how many times they chose to use the credit card and how much they actually spent. While they are convenient when you find yourself short on cash, credit card debt and their fees can quickly add up.

Overspending

After a weekend of splurging, you come to realize that you spent $1,000. Originally you had applied for the credit card "in case of an emergency." At the time, each of your purchases may very well have been an emergency (but that is a conversation we will have in the next chapter). Nevertheless, the 13.99% APR that this particular card carries can quickly put you in a position that you may not be prepared for. Since you do not have the $1,000 within your budget to pay off the entire balance at the end of the month, you now find yourself in debt.

So, your $1,000 balance will now grow every month until it is completely paid off because of the compounding nature of interest. Let's say your statement indicates a minimum payment of $50. At this rate, it will take you almost two years to pay off the debt and you will pay an additional $145 in interest. Wouldn't that money be better spent on something else or even saved to avoid a future "emergency"? Yes! I can certainly think of other things to use my money on than give it to the credit card company.

Minimum payment

Many borrowers fall into this trap of paying only the minimum amount required on the statement, keeping themselves in debt far longer than necessary and paying more than they bargained for. Instead, try to pay down this debt faster, reducing the amount of interest that accrues, and giving yourself the opportunity to use that money elsewhere.

Everyday spending

While you may have created a monthly budget to account for everyday spending, some people choose to use a credit card for common purchases such as groceries and even to pay utility bills. Unless you have built these items into your budget to allow you to pay off the credit card at the end of the month, you may find now in a position of having to pay for those expenses as well as an additional credit card payment each month.

Rewards or repercussions?

Some people may justify using the credit card as a means of collecting rewards or points. Sadly, this is a ploy by credit card companies to get you to use the card (unnecessarily) to accumulate points with the expectation that you are getting something in return. In all likelihood, you are getting something, but it is certainly not worth the money spent on the interest and fees that may also accumulate. For example, you may earn cash towards frequent flyer miles or rewards. This concept is certainly a bonus if you pay off the balance each month and avoid new debt, as you can earn discounted tickets, prizes and even cash back.

Convenience checks?

Have you ever considered using one of those convenient checks that credit card companies send in the mail? Maybe you have in fact used one. No need to be embarrassed, they are sent out for a reason. . . for people to use. They can be beneficial if, again, you pay it off quickly. For example, if you need it in an emergency until your check comes in at the end of the month. If you have done this, kudos to you! Most people unfortunately fall into the trap of using these checks and NOT paying it off, thus creating debt. These checks, although they appear to be harmless, are considered to be a cash advance on which interest begins to accrue immediately as well as an additional fee for the use of this money in advance. Do not fall victim to this ploy!! Shred the check immediately to avoid any temptations.

Medical Payments

While many people have healthcare coverage, the cost of medical care is not covered entirely by insurance. There are copays, deductibles, and unforeseen expenses. For others without insurance, the cost of seeking medical attention may prohibit them from even doing so. As tempting as it may be to place these charges on your credit card, it is not a wise decision to do. Credit card companies do not care that the charge was for medical care. All they see is that interest is owed on money used. It is a better idea to negotiate a payment plan with the healthcare provider who will not charge any interest than to burden yourself with additional debt and the stress that comes with it.

Late Payments

Lastly, let's take a look at what making a payment even just one day late can do. Credit card companies love to levy fees. Aside from the interest charges, there are fees and penalties for just about anything that you can think of including late payments. On average, you may see a late fee of $35 for each payment that is not received by the lender by the due date. With the convenience of online bill pay and scheduled payments, you should not have to rely on your memory alone to ensure that those credit cards and auto loans are paid on time. The lenders don't care that the mail is delayed either!

Remember when we talked about how simple interest is calculated and that if you pay before the due date, the amount of interest that accrues is less? The same holds true if you are late on your payment. So be aware of those dates to ensure that you do not add to your balance with additional late payment fees and higher interest charges.

Now I know that this chapter may make your head spin or maybe put you to sleep. But, it was important that we get the touchy stuff out of the way. Let's summarize what we learned.

Summary--Interest--The Devil's in the Details

- Interest is the money that you must pay to a lender for use of their money no matter the vehicle (i.e. auto loan, mortgage, student loan, credit cards)
- There are several ways that interest is calculated including fixed interest rate, variable interest rate, simple interest and compound interest, and it is important to know the method that applies to your specific debt.
- Interest and the method of calculation can be very dangerous, leading to more debt, stress and financial strain if not managed properly.

Aside from my student loan debt, I had also taken out several credit cards to help me get through what I thought were financial emergencies. What I did not understand was that as I racked up the charges on the card, my financial situation was getting more and more difficult. Because I was drowning in student loan debt, I thought that I could pay for my everyday living expenses via the credit card and simply default payment just a little while or until I got on my feet again.

Little did I know, the interest rate that I was paying on those cards was upwards of 15% and I had put myself into a nearly impossible situation. I could barely make the minimum payment each month on the existing balance and still the interest kept adding to it. Something had to give. I had to get a hold of my finances once and for all and make a commitment to controlling my behaviors and ultimately my money.

As you will read in the next chapter, there is a psychology behind the concept of money and more importantly debt. We will discuss how debt negatively affects our mind thus influencing our behavior thus perpetuating the debt cycle. Ultimately, I will reveal how I decided to spend, save, and repay those debts that were like a heavy burden.

Let's keep going.

3

DEBT PSYCHOLOGY 101

If you have picked up this book, my guess is that you are feeling the weight of debt barreling down on you. You are not alone, and this is very important to remember. Do you recall that figure that I gave you earlier about the number of people in some form of debt? 189 million. Yes, you read that correctly--189 million people are in the same position as you are! So, now that we have the loneliness out of the way, let's take a look at what other areas of your life this debt may impact.

According to scientists and medical doctors, finances play a major role in millions of people's stress levels, and ultimately mental and physical health. If you haven't figured it out yet, your physical body's health is directly related to your psychological health, and if you are stressed about money, what do you think happens?

As reported by LiveScience.com, researchers have found that "people with high stress levels (over debt) were twice as likely to have a heart attack compared with those who did not worry about their financial situation." Stress about how you are going to pay the next mortgage payment, the amount that you owe in credit card debt and of course, that large sum that you owe for your college education places so much strain on the body that oftentimes the body cannot help but to react negatively: stomach ulcers, headaches, neck or back strain to name a few.

Even if you did not experience mental health issues previously, stress can even be the trigger that launches your mind into depression and anxiety. Been feeling more than just stressed lately? Are you experiencing deep sadness, hopelessness, and despair about your financial situation? Your debt may have impacted your mind and body even more than you thought.

However, please note that in no way am I proclaiming to be a therapist, or even suggesting that I can assist with a psychological issue. I am merely suggesting that if you are experiencing any of these physical ailments or mental anguish, it may be caused by debt. While I hope that my experiences and insight will assist you in your financial journey, I highly recommend that you seek professional assistance from a medical practitioner or mental health professional if necessary.

Now it may be easy for some people to throw it out there that you should simply stop spending to get control of your debt, but in reality it is not quite that simple. Debt has you feeling stressed, uncertain about the direction to go in, and over-whelmed which, when combined, often make us do "nothing". Have you ever heard the phrase that "not making a decision is in fact making a decision?" When it comes to your finances, this could not contain more truth and, at the same time, be more detrimental to your financial, physical and mental health.

Think about it. Because you are overwhelmed and frustrated, you may not have put in the effort to get your debt under control previously. If you are like many people, you secretly hope that by ignoring the problem, it will somehow just go away. However, with the nature of debt and interest as we learned about in the previous chapter, by making late payments, minimum payments, or skipping payments altogether (which we didn't even touch on), or in other words, not making any decisions, you are consequently making a decision. Confused? You have subconsciously decided that you are not going to do anything about the debt again with the hope that if you don't see it, it will go away! I am very sorry to tell you, my friend, that that is NEVER going to happen!

Once you open your eyes and make the decision that you are going to do something about your financial situation, you have undoubtedly accrued large amounts of interest, added drastic charges in late fees, and even quite possibly brought upon repossession of your assets because of lack of payment. And you thought you had financial troubles and stress before!!!

No! Avoiding the problem is not going to alleviate the stress that you may be feeling or the mental and physical challenges. As I have told you, I had to take the bull by the horns and figure this thing out, and you can too!

So, let's get started!

DEBT PAY-OFF PLAN

There are probably as many philosophies out there about paying off debt as there are credit card companies. Well, maybe not that many, but certainly there are quite a few financial gurus who have tipped their hats as to THEIR best strategy. As I mentioned earlier, it is important that you learn as much about financial management as you can, so feel free to explore others. I just want to tell you what worked best for me.

Money-management expert Dave Ramsey has been touting for years his theory of paying off the smallest debts first. While there is merit in looking at things the other way around and paying off the highest ones first, let's look at Dave's idea first.

Dave Ramsey suggests that you should prioritize your list of debts from the smallest amount due to the highest regardless of the interest rate. There are many critics of this technique who argue that those who are in debt should pay off the ones with the highest interest rate or the highest balance first. However, researchers have determined that there are psychological benefits to Dave's theory.

According to a study in the Journal for Marketing Research, attacking the smallest debt first has a greater impact than simply reducing the debt. In fact, with each accomplishment, the brain is stimulated to keep pushing forward. It is motivated to tackle the next one and encouraged to maintain self-control.

Have you heard the phrase "eat the elephant one bite at a time?" Well, when you look at your debt from a high level, combining all of the debt into one lump sum, it can appear to be a daunting task--a giant elephant! If you were to try to "eat" this mammoth creature all at once, obviously it would be a difficult task. But what if you were to take small bites of the elephant, eating away at it little by little? Wouldn't you be encouraged to continue what you are doing if you saw that little by little you were making progress?

When you set small goals for yourself, taking one step at a time, the achievement of each goal motivates you to keep going. While the argument for paying off credit cards with the highest interest rate or the largest balance may appeal to your budget, lowering the amount of interest paid, the psychology of it makes it more difficult for the mind to accept.

Since so much of our behavior and thus spending habits stem from how we feel, doesn't it seem logical that our ability to pay off debt should also be dictated by feelings as well? If you have $100k in debt, putting all of your energy and money into paying it down quickly, you may become discouraged when the balance due only moves to $98k after months of payments. It is very easy to be side-tracked or tempted when you look at it from the elephant point of view. "I am not making much progress anyway, so it doesn't really matter if I splurge a little this month and buy myself something nice."

Look at it from Dave Ramsey's perspective. You have a $1000 balance due on a credit card and after the same number of months, your hard work and effort pay off and you have successfully repaid the amount borrowed. Imagine the sense of accomplishment that you will feel knowing that you have set a goal for yourself and met it. You will be encouraged and probably eager to get started on the next debt item in your list. You will more than likely think twice about spending on the card again and destroying all of that hard work.

This same concept works in so many areas of life. I don't want to go too far off of the subject but think about the last time you tried to lose weight (maybe you are fortunate enough that you have never had to diet--kudos to you!) But, for anyone who has set a goal to lose let's say 20 or 30 pounds, the task looms over-head and seems impossible at first. Nutritionists and fitness experts say that although you know how much you ultimately might want to lose, tackle just this week by setting a manageable goal of simply a pound or two. Don't you feel accomplished and positive when at the end of the week you have reached your goal? That boost in your mood is the motivation that many of us need to take on the next week or in our case, that next debt.

So, when developing your debt pay-off plan, it may seem logical if not even expected to tackle those debts with the highest interest rate first, psychology tells us that it is in your best interest (pun intended) to design your plan with your first priority being the debt item with the lowest balance. Although you will be focusing on reducing the item with the lowest amount of interest that accrues, it is the psychological benefits that will be impacted the most.

Just imagine the smile that will creep across your face as you write the last check for that one credit card payment! How will you feel knowing that you cross that one line item off of your budget? However, let's not get ahead of ourselves just yet thinking that you now have more more in your pocket. On the contrary, actually! According to Dave Ramsey, you take the monthly payment that you were paying to that low balance credit card and add it to the monthly payment of the next lowest balance. Do you see the possibilities? Can you feel the stress diminishing as you methodically work through each of your debts?

SPEND OR SAVE?

Now that you are feeling good, you have a little more bounce in your step and you have a more positive outlook on your finances, you may be tempted to go out and buy yourself that new watch you've had your eye on or to take a much-needed mini vacation. Have you thought about HOW you will pay for either one of these splurges? Many people experience a newfound feeling of freedom as they begin to see movement in their debt. As Dave Ramsey calls it, your debt begins to snow-ball with each payment getting larger as a smaller debt is paid off.

At this point, this freedom may get you thinking about buying that item that you have had your eye on forever, but you have to consider, at what expense? Will that shiny object fulfill a need? Will it make you feel accomplished? The bigger question is, will you actually remember what you purchased when that credit card statement arrives in the mail? For most people, the answer is a resounding NO!

While you can certainly put your finger on (literally) those big ticket items for which you carry a loan, such as your home, car, and you can even take hold of that college diploma for the education that you are still paying for, those credit card balances have a way of sneaking up on you leaving you feeling deflated and frankly, abused. This word may seem harsh but let's consider for a moment those feelings again since they seem to be the driving force behind much of our spending anyway.

How does "spending" make you feel? You might feel the exhila-ration of having something new on your wrist or in your home for a moment. But how long does that feeling last? My guess would be that by the end of the week, if not sooner, the novelty has worn off and you are on the hunt for the next "thing" to give you that warm feeling that you like so much. That feeling is often replaced by another not so fuzzy feeling called buyers' remorse when the bill comes in later that month, followed by regret, disappointment in yourself and your choices, stress over the situation, and on it goes. I used the word 'abused' intentionally, because in reality you have done just that. You have abused your finances, putting yourself into a position that will cause you additional grief, stress and mental anguish. Obviously, none of us wants to feel this way.

For a second let's circle back to a time not that many years ago when consumers "saved" money in anticipation of making a purchase. Before the age of the credit card, you had to either have enough cash to make the purchase or negotiate with the seller directly to establish a line of credit. Did the purchase make the buyer feel any differently? I am willing to bet that it did because there is value in anticipation and achieving that goal of saving the money. Think about how you will feel when you pay off that first loan. Now envision what it would feel like to save the money in advance of making the purchase. How much better will you feel and be proud of your decision knowing that you decided to save and then spend versus spend and then *not* have the ability to save!!

TEMPTATIONS ALL AROUND

Unfortunately, there are temptations all around us taunting us to use that credit card that is sitting idly in your wallet. During the time when you had to save to make a large purchase, there was certainly advertising at every corner: the shop window, the billboard on the highway, the rooftop advertisement. Some companies even place flyers on car windows and the side of milk cartons.

Today, we are bombarded with marketing ploys thousands of times per day. The neon signs, billboards, television ads, radio broadcasts, podcasts, and store circulars would be enough if it were not for the big Kahuna in temptations--the Internet! Marketing and advertising companies found a way to creep into our ear holes and eye holes to deposit little nuggets of information at every opportunity. Between the product place-ment in television ads and the video streaming on our phones and the ads that flash across the screen of our email, we receive millions of bits of data that create a desire in us. Even if it is not a conscious thought, our brains process this infor-mation and conveniently store it until the right time causing us to act spontaneously and sometimes outside of our comfort zone.

Let's not forget about social media! Your neighbor just bought a new car, your cousin put in a new pool, and your best friend is currently sipping something fruity on a beach somewhere! You can't tell me that there isn't a little bit of your psyche that isn't tickled as you passively scroll through your social media fees! Is that jealousy? Envy? Of course, from pictures alone you have no way of knowing exactly HOW each person is able to do and buy whatever it is that they want. From the outside, it does appear that each person may have suddenly hit the lottery or inherited from a great aunt!

While it might be possible that one of your friends might have inexplicably come into some cash, I would like to suggest an alternate explanation for others' ability to seemingly spend however they wish. Spend or Save? I would like to have confidence that everyone who is posting pictures of their new toys or shopping sprees has in fact saved the money to make those purchases. Unfortunately, being that the statistics of those in debt are what they are, I would be willing to guess that this is not true!

For many people, the concept of "keeping up with the Joneses" is simply too much for them to resist. Is that you? Do you always desire to have the latest and greatest technology? Do you need to have the coolest and newest fashion trends? Are you always tempted and, more importantly, do you give in to the marketing and advertising ploys of marketers? Is it important for you to always look the part, and how does this impact your spending habits?

The bottom line is that external temptations can have a tremendous amount of impact on your budget and debt situation. You may not think so but go back and read through this section again. Ask yourself those same questions again. Really think about your spending and saving habits and then take a look at your debt plan. Consider whether you have a healthy perspective on money, spending and debt.

- Are you diligent with following a plan?
- Do you maintain a healthy perspective on your finances or are you sucked in by all things that are shiny?
- Do your long-term goals outweigh your short-term needs for immediate gratification?
- Are you a spontaneous, emotional consumer?

Your response to these questions will determine your mindset about finances and should give you some idea as to where you need to make change. The psychology of debt does not simply revolve around how it makes you feel AFTER the fact, but rather it determines your philosophy and therefore, behaviors BEFORE as well. If you don't like the negative feelings and stress that stem from your financial decision, you have to decide that you are going to take control. Then you must evaluate your mindset about spending and saving and make a decision as to how you want to live your life.

Do you want to enjoy debt-free living and therefore a life without the stress and strain of your finances? Or do you prefer the rewards and satisfaction of instant gratification and ulti-mately, stress and financial burden? You DO have a choice! You can choose to holster your credit card like a dutiful soldier holsters his gun. You do not have to be ready to swipe and tap simply because you are tempted by something shiny!

Change your thoughts, change your behavior, change your life!

This chapter may have taken you on a bit of an emotional rollercoaster and that is ok. I wanted you to experience the pain and discomfort that debt places on your life and conversely, the fact that it does not have to be that way. You have control over the outcome of your life, and you can take control of your finances. You have to make the decision to do so.

SUMMARY - DEBT PSYCHOLOGY 101

- Debt places an enormous amount of stress and strain on the body both physically and mentally.
- An effective approach to a debt pay-off plan is to prioritize your debts from smallest balance to highest and aggressively pay off the smallest one first.
- Spending or saving is a mindset that can lead you to making decisions that have the potential to drastically change your financial situation one way or the other.
- It is inevitable that you will be tempted. With temptations to wield your credit card like a samurai warrior all around you, how you choose to manage these temptations will determine your financial success.

Once I decided that I was going to live a debt-free life, I became committed to achieving this goal. Like you may be, I was easily distracted by the lifestyle of others and I wanted it all NOW, even though I was already buried under a mountain of debt. I began to understand that if I was going to experience life as I wanted to, I was not only going to need to make a change in my spending habits, but more importantly, in my perspective on debt.

I sat down and immediately prioritized my debts in smallest to largest order as Dave Ramsey suggested. I then reevaluated my budget to see where I could adjust my spending. The most amazing thing happened! I paid off my very first credit card debt! I was more than elated. I felt triumphant, accomplished, and motivated. Although this credit card had a balance of just under $1000, it felt so good to say goodbye to that statement each month. I had taken one small bite of the elephant and small it was. With my overall debt balance over $100k, I decided that I could no longer avoid the fact that I was in debt.

By attacking and successfully paying down that first item, I felt encouraged to keep going and surprisingly, I felt better too. I experienced a sensation that even just a little bit of weight had been lifted from my shoulders. Now don't get me wrong! It wasn't all roses and unicorns. I was certainly tempted to go out and splurge every once in a while, throwing down my credit card at dinner as if I was Daddy Warbucks. So I want to tell you that as you begin your journey of getting your debt under control, you will make mistakes too! And that's ok! But by developing a positive mindset, changing your perspective, and being motivated by your accomplishments, I am certain that you will achieve your goals!

Remember that as I told you in the beginning, my process leading up to a debt-free life took me five years. Although it does not have to take you that long, understand that it is just that--a process. It is a change that will be uncomfortable, stressful, and yet ultimately fulfilling knowing that you were able to take charge of your debt and live your life debt free.

In the next chapter, we will take a deep dive into your expenses, and creating and sticking to a budget. You have come this far, no reason to turn back now!

STEP 2: GETTING YOUR DUCKS IN A ROW

4

TIME TO GET FRIENDLY WITH YOUR EXPENSES!

After all that we have discussed to this point, I am sure you have probably already guessed what comes next. You not only know that you want to live a debt-free life, but you have a fairly good idea as to your debt pay-off plan. If you are anything like me, you may also be pretty excited to get started. Once I realized that my financial future was in my hands, I could not wait to jump in.

However, I will also tell you that I was not as prepared as I should have been when it came to the actual process of paying off debt. I assumed that I could simply prioritize the debt, make payments as usual, and somehow there was magically going to be enough money to keep me at my standard of living AND pay down my debt. Boy was I wrong!

What I did not realize and why it is so important that I share this with you is that I had to take a good hard look at my expenses first and create a budget that I could live by. It is easy to create the budget on paper (or software if you choose to use it). The hard part is sticking to it, which requires discipline and a positive mindset.

Remember the example that I used earlier of the dieter? Just as difficult as it may be to stick to an eating regimen, it can be just as hard to follow a budget. While sustainability is the key, it doesn't make it any easier. I get it! But once you understand why it is so important to keep track of your food or in our case our expenses, you will see how with minimal effort you can make a huge impact on your life.

ACCOUNTABILITY

First things first, do you actually know where your money goes each month? As I started this book by quoting Dave Ramsey, "You've got to tell your money what to do or it will leave." If you have not been diligently keeping track of your expenses and following a budget until now, in other words, telling it what to do, your money has certainly been leaving you.

A budget is an estimate of income and expenses each month. If you are working full-time, you should have a pretty good idea about how much money you earn each month. It is the expenses that may be a bit more elusive. Unfortunately, most people just go about life earning and spending, not really understanding the full scope of their financial situation. By creating a budget, you can visually see how much money comes in the door versus how much is going out each month, week and ultimately, every day. It is an excellent way of not only seeing where your money goes but helping you to decide what you want to do with it. In other words, a budget is a means of holding you accountable to your earning and spending habits.

Although it may be as simple as pulling your pay stubs to see how much you earn, you may have to use several sources to figure out your expenses i.e. bank statements, credit card statements, PayPal transactions, Google Pay transactions. Since there are so many ways of transferring money or paying bills these days, it is important that you review each of them to make sure that you capture all of your expenses accurately. Don't forget about cash!! While cash transactions have certainly dwindled, you may still pay for small ticket items such as coffee or stamps using cash. The point is that regardless of how you pay for something, it is still considered an expenditure.

Now, earning more money may be easier said than done but certainly not impossible and should be taken into consideration when looking at your overall financial strategy. However, this is not a book about earning extra income or even career/job changes to get a bigger paycheck. No. In this book, since we are talking about specifically debt-free living, I am going to focus on living within your means or basing your budget on the money that you currently earn.

EXPENSE TRACKING

Once you have created a budget including categories for small purchases and monthly bills, it is time to take a look at it. You may be shocked (and rightfully so) when you realize how much money flies out the window each month on subscriptions and take-out. You might see that you pay multiple service providers for lawn maintenance when you might be able to consolidate to one. If you have never looked at your expenses before, you could be surprised to learn how much money you truly spend between the organic food store, the grocery store, and the farmer's market!

By tracking your expenses, you can see what percentage of your hard-earned dollars is spent in each category and how much, if any, is leftover for savings, debt repayment, and planning for the future. In a best-case scenario, there is money available for each of these categories, but for many people, savings is one area that goes unaddressed. Expense tracking allows you to make adjustments in your spending habits or even identify areas of excess to make room to pay down debt and eventually sock some money away into savings.

Have you heard the phrase, "what gets measured gets done"? In my opinion, this phrase is spot on. If you have never created a budget or looked at your expenses, you could never have hoped to have control of your finances or to know when NOT to spend. If you measure or track how your money is spent, you have a much better chance at controlling it and telling it where to go. However, if you have never done this before, do not worry. No judgment here! It is not too late to start.

CHANGES

Having a written budget allows you to not only identify where you are spending your money but also where you may need to make changes. As I mentioned earlier, you may only now recognize that each person in your home is subscribed to a different music service. Why? Each person signed up on their own to get what suits their needs. Is there a better, more cost-effective way of listening to tunes? Not only does your budget tracking system now catch those things, but it will help you to see what your finances may look like once you consolidate or terminate some of those plans.

Once you have several months of budget and expense data recorded, you may also notice certain trends or areas for improvement. For example, you may notice that your electric bill is much higher in the summer when the air conditioner is running. Although it clearly uses more energy, it may be time to consider installing a more energy-efficient unit to save on your utility expenses. It may also be a good idea to call your cable and cell phone provider on a fairly regular (semi-annual) basis to see if you qualify for any promotional rates or discounts to cut down on some of those other monthly expenses. Any changes in money going out the door will be apparent in the line items of your budget and will give you a great way of keeping track of your overall financial health.

SPENDING ISSUES

Tracking your expenses will also quickly alert you to spending issues. At first, you may not recognize a specific buying habit as an issue, but as you get more familiar with your budget and where your money goes, you will also become more sensitive to when your spending habits become toxic. You may never have considered your daily Starbucks run to be problematic. Why would you? It's just $5, right?

Let's do some simple math. $5 per day x 5 days per week x 4 weeks per month = $100 per month in coffee. WOW! Instead of spending that money on coffee, imagine what you could do to pay down your debt? Maybe $100 doesn't sound like a lot to you - how about $1200? Do I have your attention now?

$100 per month x 12 months = $1200 per year down the drain - literally speaking of course!

Now does your $5 per day coffee habit seem like a toxic habit? By tracking your expenses for any length of time, you will begin to see trends, spending habits and issues that should be addressed. Of course, it is your money and you have every right to say that $5 per day in a coffee habit is well-worth the expense. As I have been saying all along, you have a choice in the matter of what your money does. My only point is that by tracking your expenses, a clear picture of your financial situation will be revealed and you now have some choices to make.

In the example above, you may decide to continue with your Starbucks runs but maybe you can get rid of one car for a short period of time until you get control of your finances and pay-off your debt. Your debt pay-off plan and strategy for achieving your goals is completely within your control and only you can make those decisions.

ACHIEVING YOUR GOALS

A budget and expense tracking system is ultimately going to help you achieve your goals. As you learn to monitor your spending, stick to a budget, and reduce unnecessary expenses, you will also have a means of tracking your progress. As I said earlier, "what gets measured, gets done." If you never keep a record of where your money goes, you have no way of knowing if you are on track to achieve your goals or if you are failing miserably. You have no reference point and therefore, will continue endlessly accumulating debt, living in the moment with no plan for the future.

HOW TO KEEP TRACK OF EXPENSES

Now that you know the importance of tracking your expenses, the next logical question is HOW. Don't let the idea of numbers scare you as I know many of you are. The process of keeping track of your expenses can be as simple or as complicated as you make it. It all depends on your comfort level and how detailed you want to be with your numbers.

Pen and Paper

If you are new to budgeting or uncomfortable with complicated calculations, you can create a simple budget using a notebook or ledger. List categories for each of your expenditures and the monthly amount for each. At the bottom, add a line for the sum of all of the expenses and this is your total expenditure for the month. This is fairly simple for the big items such as rent, electric bill, and car note but may be more difficult to account for those small, daily expenses such as coffee and lottery tickets, but as we have discussed, they are no less important. Maintain a separatee list, maybe on the back of your paper to write down each and every one of those expenses even as insignificant as they may seem. Remember how quickly your Starbucks coffee expense added up. Have you ever started the week with $50 in your wallet to only have a few bucks left at the end of the week? I like to call this the "dribble". Money simply dribbles through your fingers unbeknownst to you. It is those seemingly insignificant expenditures that may be hampering your debt pay-off plan but again you will not know that unless you keep track of your expenses.

I digress. Keep a detailed list of all your spending so that you know exactly where your money is going. You can create additional categories based on your specific spending habits to add to your list of expenses such as groceries, coffee, entertainment, miscellaneous. These are up to you but equally as important as those regular monthly expenses.

Again, it is up to you how complicated your tracking system is, but it has to work for you. If keeping track via pen and paper sufficiently gives you the picture that you need to manage your debt, then that is all you need. However, if you want to make it more involved or even automated, there are definitely tools out there for that, too.

App or software

If you are tech savvy and want to use an app or software, you can certainly find that best suits your needs. From a simple Excel sheet to a web-based financial app and everything in between, there is a resource available to help everyone budget and track their expenses. Again, I am not here to tell you that one method is better than another. I simply want to impose on you the necessity and benefit of the process.

Let's take a look at several of the available resources:

Excel spreadsheet: easy to use and allows you to add formulas to automatically total your categories and overall expenses depending on how you set up your worksheet. Again, this process can be as simple or complicated as you are comfortable with.

Budgeting Apps: technology has given us the ability to look at our budgets and even track our expenses on a daily basis. This can be extremely beneficial if you are serious about managing your debt and your pay-off plan (which I know you are). Here are some of the top budgeting apps for 2020 according to The Balance.

- **Mint:** Best Overall
- **PocketGuard:** Best to Keep From Overspending
- **You Need a Budget:** Best for Type-A Personalities
- **Wally:** Best for Just Budgeting
- **Mvelopes:** Best for Cash Style Budgeting
- **Goodbudget:** Best for Couples
- **Simple:** Best App Tied to a Bank Account
- **Personal Capital:** Best for Investors

Software: similar to an Excel sheet, you can use a software tool to create and manage your budget and expense tracking. Many of the available tools will have built in calculations and will offer options and suggestions such as trends that it identifies. If you are a more visual person, they often provide a picture through a graph or chart of your progress and goals. Some effective tools include Quicken, Microsoft Money, and AceMoney Lite.

Many banks now offer handy tools and resources to alert you when bills are due, when expenses are incurred and when your statements are available. Use each of these as you are comfortable and understand that they ultimately will help you to reach your goals.

OVERSPENDING

One mistake that many people make when it comes to their budget and expenses is that as soon as the going gets tough, they bail out of the process. Whether you have identified a pattern of overspending or just splurged too much last month, do not be discouraged! This is the reason that you are tracking your expenses in the first place--to identify the behavior and make a change. Everyone will stumble once in a while. Remember your last diet attempt? Did you quit and throw away all of your hard work and effort over the last several months simply because you chose to have an extra glass of wine with dinner? NO--although I am sure that there are some people who might, that is not who you are. You have made the decision to embark on a journey of debt-free living and one month of overspending will not deter you from your course. Stick with your budget and use this as an opportunity to grow and move on.

This is one more reason why it is so important that you review your budget and expenses every month. If you only review it every few months or so, you are not likely to see the trends in spending and if you do, it may be too late to do anything about it. Make it a habit to sit down and review your expenses and spending habits on a regular basis so that you can catch those mistakes or correct those habits before they derail your debt pay-off or savings plan.

SUMMARY - TIME TO GET FRIENDLY WITH YOUR EXPENSES!

- Creating a budget and tracking your expenses monthly gives you the big-picture view of your overall financial situation and holds you accountable.
- You want to tell your money where to go. By tracking your expenses, you not only see where it has been going, but can now direct it accordingly.
- Tracking your expenses is critical to know where change is needed as well as the impact when you make a change.
- Identifying any spending issues or habits before they get out of hand is critical to understanding your financial situation and staying on track with your debt pay-off plan.
- Through the process of creating a budget and tracking

your expenses, you can see your progress in achieving your goals.

- Tracking expenses does not have to be complicated and can be accomplished using pen and paper or the software of your choice.

I always like to end each chapter with a little story about my own financial situation. I found that an Excel Spreadsheet has worked very well for me. I can create or change categories to fit my needs and I have even added due dates of many of my bills and debts to help me to manage my money more efficiently. I even added a simple calculation to estimate a pay-off date for each of my loans so that I can work toward those goals and track my progress.

I cannot stress enough the importance of using a budget and tracking system that works best for you. If it is overly complicated or difficult, most people will quickly abandon it. Just like any diet and exercise routine, it has to be sustainable and manageable for most people to stick with it. There is no need to overcomplicate the process or make it so that it requires hours each month for you to track your expenses. Keep it simple!

Although it may seem a bit overwhelming now, I guarantee that once you get started and have several months of tracking under your belt, you will see the impact in your financial situation and honestly, your perspective on it as well. Part of getting control over your expenses is simply being aware. As I mentioned earlier, if you were not aware that your $5 per day coffee habit was costing you $1200 per year, you may never have changed it. Tracking expenses gives you the ability to see how your spending habits today can greatly impact your financial situation in the future. Why not get hold of it now rather than look back with regret in the future if you do not achieve your desired financial goals!

In the next chapter, we will get into greater detail about how to develop your master plan, including creating your budget, what expenses to track, how to slim down your spending, and the best way to tackle your debt.

5

THE MASTER PLAN: LET'S CREATE IT

Are you ready? Hopefully by now, you should have a pretty good idea as to what we will be covering in this chapter--The Master Plan. In other words, the exact steps that you need to take the bull by the horns and get your debt under control once and for all. I want to remind you as we move forward that, as Dave Ramsey says, "debt is not the boss of your money. You are."

Without further ado, let's get started.

In the last chapter, we talked about several methods of keeping track of your expenses including good old pen and paper, Excel, or an online application. Whatever works best for you right now, know that you can change your methodology once you get comfortable with the process and/or want to get a little more detailed. For the sake of ease, let's look at the middle road and use an Excel sheet to keep an accounting of income and expenses and to look at the big picture of your finances.

STEP 1:

Start by obtaining the last three months of bank statements. This will give you a good overview of what your spending habits have been over the last several months as well as help you to identify any trends, unusual expenses, or even ghost expenses that I'll talk about in a minute.

Most banks now offer customers the ability to download statements into a CSV file that you can then import into an Excel sheet if you are technically savvy enough. If this is a little too complicated for you, feel free to use the paper copy that your bank mails you each month and enter each line item into the Excel sheet with its appropriate amount. You want to capture all expenses from the bank statement as this is a true record of the ins and outs of where your money goes. Of course, it will not account for any expenses that you pay via cash, but we will address that shortly as well.

STEP 2:

Assign each line item to a specific category. Now although this may sound complicated, it can be as simple or complicated as you want it to be. For example, you may choose to lump expenses such as coffee, subscriptions and bank fees into a "miscellaneous" category, as long as you understand that you risk losing the visibility to where your money may be "leaking" out the door, as I like to call it. On the other hand, you may want to have separate categories for some of those items so that you can capture how much money you actually spend on coffee per year as we talked about earlier.

Examples of common categories:

- Auto (Auto loan/maintenance/fuel)
- Home (Mortgage/rent/)
- Home maintenance (lawn service/snowplow)
- Entertainment (could include dining out, movies, bowling, or whatever you deem as entertaining)
- Groceries
- Health/Personal Care (Doctor visits/co-pays, therapy)
- Pets
- Insurance
- Utilities (oil/gas/electric, water, trash)
- Telephone/cable/internet
- Credit card debt
- Charity
- Miscellaneous (as mentioned, this category can be as focused or broad as you like to include subscriptions, fees, dry cleaning, shopping, home goods, etc.)

The purpose behind assigning each item to a category is so that you can calculate the total for each category each month, compare it to previous months, as well as calculate the average spent. This calculation will help you to create a budget using the average dollar amount spent per month as well as catch any significant changes (positive/negative) that may occur.

STEP 3:

Sort each transaction by its assigned category and use a function to sum the expenses in that category.

If you can, use a function to calculate the average of the three months.

STEP 4:

On the same Excel sheet, or if necessary, a new one, enter all of your sources of income for the month. If you have a fairly regular stream of income, this should be relatively easy to calculate. If on the other hand, you work gig work, have your own business, or otherwise have irregular income, it may be more difficult to manage your budget and debt pay off plan, but certainly not impossible.

STEP 5:

Using the income from the last three months' statements, calculate the total income earned in each month and then also calculate what your average monthly income for the three months is.

This will give you an idea as to how much you are working with to allocate towards expenses, your debt payoff plan, and your emergency fund which we will discuss in detail in the next chapter.

Ghost Expenses

Before we go any further into the Master Plan, let's take a look at those expenses which we will refer to as "ghost expenses". They are the subtle, almost inconsequential expenses that have the possibility of eroding your well-thought-out debt pay-off plan and derailing your budget in any given month.

You may have categorized them under miscellaneous because you were not really sure where to put them or in some cases, what they are. It is time to go back to your spreadsheet and even your bank statement to take a look at those possibly unrecognizable expenditures. You may be wondering when the last time you read a book via Audible.com, used your Active.com membership or earned those bonus points for a video subscription you didn't know you had. You are not alone. As it has been increasingly easier to register online for nearly anything we want, many of us find ourselves plugging in our credit card information for things that we not only don't need but we quickly forget about. Until...

Until you hunker down and get serious about your debt, it will continue to hang over you, possibly hurting you emotionally and mentally. Think about the amount of money that you very well may be unknowingly spending each month because you have forgotten about them or didn't realize that the "trial period" had expired. Unless you carefully monitor your expenses and credit card statements, you might be spending a significant chunk of money that could be used toward your debt pay off.

Let's look at an example:

A standard monthly subscription to Audible.com is $14.95. Although it was a great idea to subscribe in order to listen to audiobooks during your morning commute, you have since lost interest. Unfortunately, though, you have forgotten to cancel the subscription. Of course, the company is not going to say, "Hey, you haven't listened to a book in a while. Do you want to continue your subscription?" No way! They don't care if you ever use the service or not. They've got your money. What if you do not look at your bank statement for five months? That is $74.75 that you did NOT tell what to do but should have. That money could have been applied toward your debt payoff plan rather than lining the pocket of some unknown CEO. But I digress.

In the digital world that we live in, there are literally millions of these types of subscriptions that unsuspecting customers sign up for with the best of intentions. Consumers can order everything from media to meals to razors via a subscription-based program. While I am not suggesting that you should not subscribe or utilize these services, I am telling you that you must be mindful to unsubscribe and cancel them when they are no longer being used. These ghost charges will remain on your card or pull directly from your bank account if you are not careful to do so, and the expenses can add up quickly.

What about those items that you have on auto delivery? You suddenly receive a box of vitamins or makeup at your home having forgotten that it was on automatic delivery. For many people, they may no longer use or want the product and have neglected to notify the company. What do you do? Do you keep it and say "oh, well, I'll notify them before the next shipment or maybe even I'll return it tomorrow?" You and I both know that tomorrow never really happens when it comes to these things. Life gets busy and once again you have forgotten to cancel or return the item and you wind up with these phantom charges on your bank statement or credit card once again. How much money do consumers spend each year on products that they no longer need? Although it is difficult to calculate since most people are probably not willing to admit that this happens to them, just do a simple poll among your friends. I would be willing to bet at least half of them will tell you that they have found charges on their bank statements for items that they no longer wanted, needed, or completely forgot about.

STEP 6:

Be sure to review your statement carefully to identify any of these ghost expenses and cancel where necessary. You may even find that some of them may be useful IF utilized instead of another service, but choose wisely. For example, you may discover that you have unknowingly subscribed to several music streaming options such as Spotify AND Amazon Music. Do you really need both? More than likely not, so save yourself the money by cancelling one and apply those funds to your debt pay off plan to help you crush your debt.

Nonessentials

As reported by USA Today, "the average adult in the USA spends $1,497 a month on nonessential items, according to research commissioned by Ladder and conducted by OnePoll. All told, that's roughly $18,000 a year on things we can all do without." What does this word nonessential really mean? By definition, it means something that is not absolutely necessary. In my opinion, and certainly of most others, this definition can be interpreted in many ways. To the mother of four, music streaming services are definitely put into the nonessential category while to her children who rely on music to get them through their studies, they beg to differ. A coffee drinker will argue that his morning cup o' joe is necessary for life while the non-coffee drinker will say that it is nonessential.

The subjective nature of these purchases makes it difficult to determine if they should be eliminated from your expenses or not. My best advice when you come across these items or categories in your bank statements, you must really evaluate whether they are essential to your well-being if not at least your financial well-being. For example, do you need to purchase an expensive bottle of water every day on your way to work? What if you brought your own reusable water bottle instead? How would that impact your well-being? Probably not at all. What effect would it have on your financial well-being? At $2.50 per day, you could crush your debt even faster with an additional $50 per month applied toward it.

Most people do not even realize where their money may be leaving them until they sit down and really take a hard look at their expenses.

If you are reading this book, my assumption is that you are NOT living a debt-free lifestyle but want to. While many people think that they are drowning in debt and don't have enough money to get out from under it, in reality, they very well might be just that they have not been managing their expenses and accounting for them properly. If you can wrap your head and your spending habits around the very important steps addressed above, you might just find out that you have had the power all along to get it under control. I do not say that to make you feel badly or to have you look at the past with any regrets. You cannot change the past but you can move forward closer to a life of debt-free living if you are willing to make some hard choices and tough decisions, and I know that deciding what is essential versus nonessential may be difficult for some people.

However, keep in mind what your end goal is. If you truly want to live the life that you want, debt-free, then you will need to change some things now to get to where you want to be later. That might include making yourself even a tad uncomfortable for a short while now so that you can truly enjoy life later. On the other hand, if you have no debt and a healthy savings, then by all means splurge on those nonessential items.

STEP 7:

So, in looking at your nonessential spending, only you can decide what is nonessential or in fact essential to your well-being. If you are serious though about living a debt-free life, you know that you have to take a hardline and cut out everything except for the basic essentials such as housing, auto, groceries, insurance and utilities. If it is just too difficult to go cold turkey and cut out all nonessentials, then at least make the commitment to eliminating 50% of them. As I have been suggesting, there are other options to most things that people consider essential. For example, rather than spending $25 for a manicure, try painting your nails yourself; make coffee at home and bring it to work in a thermos or insulated cup; consolidate the music streaming options down to one account that everyone can share.

After taking care of your essentials and eliminating at least some of the nonessentials and the ghost expenses, the expectation is that you will see additional money in your budget that you can now tell what you want it to do. Remember that the whole point of this book and your goal is to crush your debt to live debt-free. I don't want to call it "extra" money because that usually implies to people that they have money to spare and ultimately spend. No! The whole idea behind evaluating your expenses and income is to identify areas in which you have not been allocating your money properly and to redirect it to what is going to get you to your goal faster.

Decision-Making time

The next part of your Master plan requires some decision making. Of the money that you have identified as "additional" in your budget and expense evaluation, break this down into three categories into which you will direct your money moving forward: 75% toward crushing your debt; 15% into an emergency fund (to be discussed shortly); and 10% towards rewarding yourself for sticking to the plan.

How you use this 10% is obviously up to you. But it is important that you still have some fun along the way. I can tell you that sticking to your Master Plan may not be easy, but it will be worth it. As you begin to see your hard work pay off, it is critical to keep yourself motivated by rewarding yourself even just a little bit. Maybe you spend that 10% on a manicure or a movie or just that coffee you are craving. Whatever it is that makes you feel good, treat yourself and keep going.

STEP 8:

We have talked about the psychology of debt and motivations. There are two ways of looking at this next step, both revolving around your motivation and optimism in achieving your goal.

1. You are highly motivated to live a life debt-free and are optimistic that you can do so if you put in the effort. Apply the money that you have allocated as going toward debt pay off to debt with the HIGHEST interest rate.

2. You are highly motivated to enjoy debt-free living but may not be as optimistic that you can do so. Begin paying off the debt with the LOWEST interest rate.

While each method has its pros and cons and both will get you to your ultimate goal, it is your perception and perspective that will make all the difference. By paying off small debts quickly, you will feel a sense of accomplishment and can help to create momentum to crush the remaining debt. It also helps to reduce stress and anxiety as the list of debts begins to decrease.

Of course, there are similar methods that will also get you to the same result: Putting all of your effort into the debt with the highest or lowest balance has the same effect. Which strategy you choose will be determined by your motivation to get it done and your perspective on how successful you will be.

SUMMARY - THE MASTER PLAN--LET'S CREATE IT

- Capture all of your expenses in an Excel sheet or software application
- Categorize each item based on type of expense
- Calculate the totals for each month by category as well as a 3-month average
- Take a look at your average income for the month
- Identify any ghost expenses and cancel/terminate where appropriate
- Evaluate categories and expenses that may not be essential to your well-being and eliminate or reduce to free up money to apply toward your debt reduction plan
- Determine the strategy that you will use and which debt you will work on reducing first

As I developed my Master Plan to get out of debt, I was highly motivated to live a life debt-free and I was VERY optimistic that I could achieve this goal. I followed the strategy of attacking those debts with the highest interest rates first. Let me tell you. It was not easy at first to cut out some of those things that I thought I needed in my life; the Happy Hour out with the boys on Friday night; the Netflix subscription and the movie channel on my cable service, and the expensive gym membership (I changed gyms to ensure that I still got my workout in, just without all of the bells and whistles of a fancy gym). As I watched the balances wither away and realized that I was not as distraught about cutting some things out of my life as I had thought, I got even more excited and motivated to keep pushing toward my goal.

I know that taking a hard look into your spending habits may be uncomfortable and may bring on feelings of guilt and regret. But as I mentioned earlier, you cannot change the past. You can only look optimistically toward the future which I see as bright and full of promise.

Now that I am living debt-free, I treat myself to the occasional night out with the guys. I still go to the same no-frills gym ,though, because my efforts demonstrated to me where my priorities lie and what I value more in my life. In order to continue living a debt-free life, I live within my means, I tell my money what I want it to do, and I have an emergency fund!

And you will do it too!

6

EMERGENCY FUND: SAVING FOR THE RAINY DAY... OR A FEW

By now you should be very comfortable with the terminology I have been using, such as expenses, debt, and interest and gotten a grasp of the big picture of your overall financial well-being. One thing I haven't touched on much is the word budget. Sure, I have used this word frequently, but I haven't really explained what it means.

To many people the idea of budgeting is a means of limiting their fun or restricting their lifestyle. While some of that may be involved, the idea of developing and sticking to a budget is simply a means of getting you to a goal. It is a spending plan that allows you to live within your means, to eliminate the stress and anxiety that comes with overextending yourself, and affords you the ability to actually make decisions about how and where you spend your money. In reality, a budget offers you freedom rather than acting as a chain that binds you as some may think.

That being said, it is important to note that while you are working on your master plan to pay off debt and live debt-free, you must also plan for the unexpected. Unfortunately, credit cards have been used for what people call "emergencies". In many cases, those emergencies have occurred as a result of poor planning or the lack of having a budget.

Let's look at an example.

You are going about your life, spending what you earn, living in the moment and not caring about the future. Suddenly, your car breaks down and the automotive repair shop informs you that it is going to be $500 to fix it. Obviously, you need your car to get to work and to carry you around town to all of your outings (nonessential I might add). It is a no brainer that since you do not have $500 sitting around in an account somewhere, you will have no choice but to use a credit card to get your car back. It is an emergency, right?

So, now that you are back in the car and on your way, you quickly forget about HOW you were able to resolve the emergency at hand. Until the credit card statement arrives next month and you realize that your lack of planning and setting any money aside for emergencies has now cost you more than the repair itself because of the interest that has accumulated on the transaction. Now let's say that because it was an unexpected expense, you do not necessarily have the "extra" money required to pay off the whole thing that first month but rather in small increments over the next six months. Not only will the interest continue to accrue but you still do not have the funds to begin planning for another unexpected event.

Let me remind you that life happens and whether you like it or not, the unexpected will and always does happen. People lose their jobs, they get sick, appliances break, and accidents happen. You have to plan for the unexpected ahead of time so as not to put yourself in a position that you have to stress, worry or make difficult decisions.

I have a friend who likes to live the way that SHE wants. She does not want to be restricted by a budget and has the mindset that she will worry about tomorrow when it arrives. She chooses not to limit her "nonessentials" because to her, they are all essential to her mental and physical well-being. She was becoming more and more burdened by her increasing debt but refused to see how her spending habits and perspective were causing her frustration and stress.

Until disaster struck. On her way to work one morning, she was involved in a minor car accident. While no one was injured, her car had significant damage. The insurance deductible was $1500. On the same day, her son fell off the monkey bars at school breaking his arm. Per her insurance policy, she was responsible for his medical bill until she met her deductible which, because her family was relatively healthy, (thankfully) she had not yet met for the year. The bill for his hospital visit was $1200.

Because of a lack of an emergency fund, my friend had no choice but to pay both of these bills with her credit card to the tune of $2700. Had she invested in her future by setting aside some money in an "emergency" fund", she may not have now found herself in a difficult position with difficult decisions to make. Now with this debt looming over her head, she finally realized that her lack of planning left her in a challenging situation both in the moment and for the future. She now had to dig her way out of debt AND develop a plan to ensure that it did not happen again.

EMERGENCY FUND

During the global pandemic during which time many people have found themselves either with no job to go to or their opportunities to earn a living so severely cut that they are now in difficult financial situations. Millions of Americans have filed for unemployment as the virus torments the economy and threatens the stability of generations. For many, who may live hand to mouth ordinarily, the crisis has left them wondering where they will find the money to feed their families tomorrow. Mortgage companies have offered forbearance, auto loan companies have allowed for borrowers to skip a payment or two. These unprecedented times have left unsuspecting and unprepared borrowers fearful of their mounting debt, concerned about their future employment, and terrified for the well-being of their families.

Under normal circumstances, having an emergency fund is designed to hedge the risks associated with everyday life as in some of the examples I have previously given such as accidents, repairs and medical emergencies. The idea behind an emergency fund is to have enough cash on hand (or liquid) that a person can access when the need arises rather than to be dependent upon the use of a credit card to bail them out of a jam. With an emergency fund, what some may consider to be a "jam" may be just a blip on the screen for others.

For many people who have found themselves unemployed during the pandemic, an emergency fund may be the difference between homelessness and sustainability. If you are living paycheck to paycheck without any "extra" stashed away for a rainy day, when that day (or many days) comes, stress and anxiety of not having options can wreak havoc on even the most logical of people.

Ultimately, whether it is a pandemic, an illness, death of a loved one, or some other reason, a rainy day always comes. It is imperative that you are forward-thinking and plan for when it does. You may be thinking, what if that rainy day never happens? If that is the case, then I want to tell you how truly lucky you are. However, as the recent global situation has revealed, anything is possible, and the future is certainly unknown. Then your emergency funds will go unused and you can consider it to be a part of your legacy that you pass down to your children. On the other hand, if you do find yourself in a position some day when you have to rely on the funds in your emergency account, that too is a lesson and legacy for future generations that with proper planning and diligence it is possible to prepare for those unexpected changes in income, life situations, or even a global pandemic--let's hope that we don't experience another one for 100+ years again!

HOW MUCH TO SAVE

At this point in your life and after evaluating your overall financial health, you may believe that there is no possible way to establish an emergency fund AND pay off your debt. However, in the last chapter, we looked carefully at the means by which you can "find" the money necessary to live debt-free as well as the formula that is recommended to accomplish it.

The question is not how much should you put into an emergency fund but rather when will you begin? The answer is NOW! Aside from college education, home mortgages and auto loans, debt in the form of consumer debt may have been avoidable with proper planning and decision-making. So, I ask you, if you were able to make the decision to purchase that new $900 television via a credit card, couldn't you also decide NOT to purchase it? Couldn't you decide to put 75% of your "extra" money toward debt and 15% toward a savings plan? While the new television may provide instant gratification, just imagine how you will feel knowing that you can pay for the much-needed repairs to your car without having to go into additional debt to do so.

So, let's look at this figure a bit more closely. Although 15% does not sound like a lot of money, of course it is relative to your income and overall financial state. For ease of calculations, I want to use $100 as the amount of money that you have been able to make available in your budget by eliminating nonessentials and ghost expenses. Of that $100, you will apply $75 toward your debt, $15 toward your emergency fund, leaving you $10 to splurge on the trip to the ice cream shop this month as a reward for your persistence.

For the sake of this conversation, I want to focus only on the $15 that you will apply to an emergency fund. Your first thought as was mine may be, what difference is $15 going to make? Well, after 12 months, your emergency fund would have $180 in it. Again, you may think, how is that going to solve any major crisis that may arise? While $180 may not seem like anything more than a drop in the bucket, it is a start.

Let's say you run over a nail in the street and puncture your tire. The auto mechanic tells you that the tire is not salvageable, and you need to purchase a new one. Which is a better decision since you clearly need your car to get to work? Purchase a new tire for $120 using your emergency fund or put this amount on a credit card at 13.99%? Without doing the math any further, the logical choice would be to pay for the tire out of your emergency savings account.

JUMP-START

Setting money aside for your emergency fund should not be a struggle as many people perceive it to be. In most cases, all you have to do is start. You will be amazed at how quickly the funds will add up with very little effort. If you are fortunate enough to earn some extra money, or receive an unexpected bonus, do not go out and spend it on just any whim. Take this opportunity to jump-start your emergency fund savings plan to better prepare yourself for those unexpected occasions. If money came to you unexpectedly, there is no better time to put money aside for the unexpected as well. What about a gift of money or your tax refund? These are both excellent ways to fund your emergency account and get a jump on those unforeseeable events that life throws at us to keep us down.

As I said earlier, life happens, and it is inevitable that at some point in your life you will run into a situation that you simply could not plan for. Although you may not be able to plan for the event itself, the best that you can do is ensure that you are financially prepared to handle it and reduce and/or eliminate any additional stress from an already stressful situation.

SUMMARY - EMERGENCY FUND--SAVING FOR THE RAINY DAY... OR A FEW

- Life throws curveballs at you and if you are not financially prepared, you may find yourself in more debt or succumb to more stress and frustration.
- As we have seen in recent times, rainy days are inevitable.
- An emergency fund is just that--money set aside in case of an emergency, however you may define it!
- How much you save in your emergency fund is dependent upon your financial situation, but I recommend 15% of your disposable income.
- Any money that you receive unexpectedly is a great way to jump-start your emergency fund to hedge against those things that occur unexpectedly.

By now you know my routine. I give you all of the nuggets of information that you need and then I share with you how I did it or the impact that it had. So, why break the routine now?

While I was struggling under the mountain of debt that I had accumulated, when I thought that my financial situation could not get any worse, I experienced a further set back. My dog, whom I love dearly, ate something he found in the yard that was apparently moldy, unbeknownst to me. Apparently, mold is toxic to dogs, which I found out when the vet handed me a

$1700 invoice to pump his stomach and inject him with anti-seizure medication. This was certainly one of those things that I had not planned for, nor was I in a financial position to lay out $1700 in cash.

It was a no-brainer that I had to pay the bill to take my dog home with me that day, but I wish the additional stress could have been left at the vet's office. Just what I needed - another payment added to my already massive credit card debt. I was stuck between a rock and a hard place, knowing that my dog's health was important to me yet not entirely sure how I was going to pay for the medical attention he received. Lacking an emergency fund, unfortunately, I only had one option.

Although not everyone would have considered this an emergency, as I mentioned, this term itself is subjective. It was an emergency that I needed to handle and using a credit card was my lifeline at the time. This is when I realized that not only did I have to put the effort into eliminating my debt for good but I also had to put in the effort to establish an emergency fund to account for those unexpected events in life. Even if it meant putting a little less money toward my debt pay off plan every month, I had to find room in my budget to set money aside.

Within several months, I had put $1000 into my emergency fund and then tax time rolled around. My $900 federal refund went straight into this account as well, giving me a little boost in savings towards the rainy day that I now knew was inevitable. Although I had no idea that a pandemic was soon going to barrel down on the world, that emergency fund has proven more helpful than I could have even imagined. It will help you too! All you have to do is get started.

In the next chapter, I will give a very helpful strategy to guide your spending and saving habits to help you achieve debt-free living.

STEP 3: CRUSHING DEBT FOREVER!

7

ENVELOPE SYSTEM: BACK TO BASICS

You have heard my stories throughout this book about my own struggles with debt and the things that I did to overcome it. I want to take a second to encourage you. It probably has not been easy to this point and it will not be easy moving forward, but if I can do it, I know that you can too! I was never the best at managing my finances until I got serious, and I never really put any thought into where my money went or how I had control over it. Money to me was simply a mechanism by which I got stuff and lived life.

It was not until I got serious about debt-free living that I came to appreciate the hard work that is required to earn money and the effort required to direct its use appropriately. Believe me, I now know that it is hard work to do both. However, I can tell you that your efforts will reap a reward once you reach your goal. When you make that final college loan payment or cut up those credit cards for good, the feelings of joy and satisfaction that you will experience will be well worth the nights spent budgeting, evaluating your spending, and limiting your transactions. It all sounds so grim as you are going through the steps that I have laid out but let me remind you of your goal: Debt-Free Living!

So, let's look at a system that I used to help make the process easier and not feel like a burden. We are going to go back to the basics of spending only what you have. We have discussed extensively that for many of us, the root of our debt problems is the ease of spending itself. Credit cards have made it simple to go to any store and purchase whatever you want. Even worse, you can sit in front of your computer and shop for ANYTHING that you want and have it in your hands as soon as the next day. Talk about a disaster waiting to happen. I would be willing to bet that if we were to look at the amount of credit card debt that many Americans have accrued since the onset of COVID-19, we would be astounded and maybe even horrified. Even if a person did not typically overspend before, they were bound to be enticed to shop more while sitting at home under Stay-At-Home orders.

During the global pandemic, the fact that nearly everything you need and want was available with a few clicks of a mouse, made staying at home almost bearable for many people. For others, it more than likely has thrown their budgets off-kilter and pushed their debt through the roof as they clicked away and simply added to their virtual shopping carts. The idea of using cash has been pushed to the wayside as businesses are pushing for contactless payments as the world slowly reopens. Although these have been troubling times and you may have taken a step backwards in your debt pay off plan because of them, rest assured that you can get back up, dust yourself off and keep moving forward.

CASH AS A BUDGETING TOOL

The reason that I brought up the recent global pandemic and credit cards is to demonstrate how easy it can be to rack up a ton of debt and to spend outside of your budget even if you do not mean to. It is much simpler to just pull out the old credit card than it is to only spend what you have. This is where cash comes in very handy as a budgeting tool.

There is no better way to keep yourself accountable than to only spend what you have. In other words, if you go to the mall with $100 in your pocket, then you know that that is your budget and you will be more conscious about your buying decisions based on this fact. The same concept applies for expense in your life. If a teenager only has $25 to spend for the week on gas, eating out and breakfast, then he or she better learn quickly how to manage his or her spending habits. Cash has a powerful way of holding us accountable and making us responsible for our decision-making and spending habits.

ENVELOPE SYSTEM

Which leads me into a unique and very simple way of managing your money and sticking within the budget that you have worked so diligently to create for yourself. It is a hands-on method for controlling your spending to ensure that you have the money available to apply toward your debt pay off plan while guaranteeing that you will not continue to incur additional debt.

So, how does the Envelope System work? The idea is that once you identify the amount of your discretionary spending each month or pay period, you withdraw this amount of cash from the bank. You would then utilize an envelope for each category of spending and label each envelope accordingly. Let's look at an example of Bill's envelope system. He receives his paycheck by direct deposit on a bi-weekly basis. Therefore, he is going to look at his spending and expenses on this same time frame and budget accordingly. Remember that the goal is to reduce all nonessential expenses to ensure that you are applying the largest sum of money toward your debt pay off plan. What you consider as essential may be different than what Bill does in our example.

- Dining out $100
- Groceries $150
- Haircut $20
- Pet food $15

- Coffee $10
- Total: $295

So, if Bill is using his envelope system appropriately, he will withdraw $295 from his bank account and place the amounts above in each envelope. When Bill goes to the supermarket, he will bring along his envelope of cash designated for groceries to pay for his purchases. Assuming that Bill does not want to overspend, he will limit the number of trips he makes to the coffee shop on the way to work based on his budget of $10 for coffee. In other words, when the money runs out in that particular envelope, you must wait until the next pay period to replenish your envelopes again.

Before we became so heavily dependent upon digital EVERY-THING, I would have suggested to you that you withdraw ALL of your income each period and allocate it accordingly by labeled envelope to be distributed. However, most of us now have automatic and/or direct payments set up for payment processing. For example, you probably do not have to write a check for your car payment or mortgage but rather send it electronically to the lender. In this case, it would not make sense to remove the cash from your account to put it in an envelope. Although, this type of payment processing makes it even more critical that you regularly monitor your bank transactions and statements to ensure that you know exactly where your money is going.

The system that I am talking about is best served for those expenses that you cannot pay online, such as the electric bill, insurance payment, or even the credit card bill. I would recommend it for the dog's grooming service, the occasional car wash, the spontaneous trip to the nail salon if these nonessentials are considered part of your budget. By using the envelope system, you will ensure that you do not spend what you do not have no matter how you categorize your spending habits.

Now, you may be tempted to consolidate all of the money that should be separated by spending category into one envelope or even dip into one of the others if you fall short in one area. I will caution you against doing this because then in reality, you are not sticking to a budget with the ability to keep track of each of your expenses. For example, let's say you decide that although you only have $30 left in your dining out budget, you want to go out with friends this Friday night and you know that it will cost you $50 at a minimum. What is the harm in taking that extra $20 from the grocery money? Well, several things: 1) You now have $20 less to spend in groceries and 2) You have broken the rule of spending what you have. While it may not be a big deal to have $20 less to spend toward groceries, it is your perception about money and your debt pay off plan that most concerns me.

Let's look at an alternate scenario. What if when you realized that you have $30 left in your dining out envelope, you decided to NOT go out at all? What would happen to that money?

Would you apply it to groceries? Would you go out and splurge on something for yourself? Would you choose to order in using just the $30 that you have? Of course, these are all options, but what if instead you applied that "extra" money toward your debt pay off plan or even your emergency fund?

Just imagine for a second what it would feel like to spend below your budget and make efficient use of that "extra" money. In reality, in a year from now or let's be realistic, in a month from now, you will not remember the missed night out with the guys but you will see the impact on your debt and savings. You might be thinking again, what will an additional $30 do for my debt when it is so huge? Consider if you remain diligent and goal oriented and you spend less than your original budget each pay period or month. The "extra" could be $30 this week, $40 the following and maybe just $5 in the third. You have now paid down $75 toward your debt that you had not expected to. Every little bit counts, so do not discount the benefits of not spending the money that you have budgeted for.

ADVANTAGES OF THE ENVELOPE SYSTEM

The beauty of the envelope system is that it really works. Financial guru Dave Ramsey has been sharing this method with his clients for years, because he has demonstrated its effectiveness if you stick to it.

As you look at your overall financial health, you may have realized that part of your debt problem was the result of having the ease of whipping out a credit card whenever possible. We have discussed the danger and detriment that this method of payment can have on even the most diligent spender's pocket. Because you have no immediate visibility to how much you have spent, you could easily rack up a hefty bill in just a few short hours and not even realize it. However, when you are using cash to pay for both essentials and nonessentials, it forces you to be more disciplined and to only spend what you have. When the cash is gone, it is time to go home!

Although we live in a digital world, think about the benefit of having actual cash on hand. During a recent storm, the power went out at my home. Not only did I lose electricity, but the entire town was out as well. This was not a problem in and of itself. However, as you heard the roar of the generators as everyone kicked them on, there was also the panic about gas to operate them. I quickly grabbed the gas can and jumped into the car. After driving to several stations to find them also without power, I managed to find one a few miles away that was lucky enough to be able to run the pumps but unfortunately could not process credit cards. Ugh! When most people walk around these days with little to no cash in their pocket, this was not a problem for me. I have been using the envelope system to budget for my gas expenses for some time now so I simply waltzed past all of the other customers, paid the attendant with cash from my envelope, and filled my gas can. Oh, the feeling of accomplishment when I was able to meet an immediate need knowing that I had the cash on hand during this crisis.

The idea of money has become somewhat nebulous for many people in that we do not necessarily have it in our hands. We swipe, tap, and transfer so frequently that we forget the reality of having to work for it and that it does run out. Using a system by which you only pay using cash brings you back to reality in the tangible nature of having a finite spending capability.

Have you ever looked at your bank account and could not figure out where the money went at the end of the month? If you recall, we talked about this early on in this book as for many people, their money simply disappears. Well, by now you know that it does not walk away on its own but in essence it does disappear because of incorrect management. When you follow the envelope system, you will find that you will know exactly where all of your money goes and more than likely will spend less overall. Because you have to consciously make a decision for each and every purchase, you are less likely to overspend or to purchase things that you don't really need.

Lastly, the envelope system of cash helps you to become laser-focused on your categories of spending. Your budget and spending habits are fluid. In other words, what may be important today may no longer be necessary in the future or at a different stage in your life. For example, you may have set aside money each week for haircuts for you and your son. During this time at home and trimming your own hair, you realize that you no longer need to visit the barber every two weeks but instead can do it yourself just fine (this may have something to do with the thinning and receding that occurs for some of us!) Nevertheless, you no longer need to have as much money in your envelope to pay for haircuts for two of you. So, what do you do with the "extra" money? Well, the best option would be to apply it toward your debt pay off plan. However, it may be a good time to reevaluate your spending categories and envelope allocations.

SUMMARY - ENVELOPE SYSTEM: BACK TO BASICS

- Spending only what you have is key when it comes to sticking to your budget and paying down debt.
- Using cash to pay for nonessential items will help you to stay within your budget and not incur any additional consumer debt.
- The envelope system is a simple method of appropriately categorizing expenses and allocating money in the form of cash to pay for each. When there is no money left in the envelope, there is nothing left to spend.
- When you do not spend all of the money in your envelope, you should apply any "extra" money toward

your debt pay off plan or in establishing your
emergency fund. A little goes a long way.

- Aside from helping you to control your spending,
  having cash on hand can help you when those
  unforeseen events occur.

I have given you a few examples throughout this chapter
already about my own use of the envelope system, but I just
want to give you one more. When I originally evaluated my
finances, established my budget and created my envelope
system, I thought that it would be a good idea to have an envelope for clothing. Each pay period the money in this envelope
would sit there unused and yet I would continue to fund it with
cash each time I went to the bank. After several months, I realized that the amount of cash in my clothing envelope had
amassed to several hundred dollars. Not only was I elated
because I now had money to move into an emergency fund, but
I also took the opportunity to adjust my system and apply that
amount to my debt payoff plan moving forward. It was clear to
me that I didn't need to purchase new clothes as often as I had
thought, therefore, changing my spending habits and freeing up
more money in my budget to get me to my goal of living debt-
free even faster.

8

IT'S GAME TIME!: STICK TO
THE PLAN

We have covered a lot of topics in this book and at this point you are either excited to get started or ready to run for the hills! While my hope is obviously the former, I completely understand any trepidation that you may be experiencing. I have been there, and I want you to know that if I could follow the process that I have outlined for you and have become debt-free, you can too. I was probably the last person who I ever thought would live my life how I want it, but ultimately, among my group of friends, I am ironically the only one who is living debt-free.

What a great feeling it is to know that I am in control of my life today and in the future. It is empowering to know that my hard work in fully embracing my debt pay-off plan has now given me the freedom to vacation when and where I want, to go out to eat if I choose to do so, and to create a nest egg for myself so that I can retire someday and continue to enjoy my life. I would not have the confidence in any of this had I not decided to take the bull by the horns when I did and take control of my finances and debt.

FOR COUPLES

For many people, conversations about money and finances are scary business. Unfortunately, money issues can impact every area of your life unless managed properly and openly discussed. According to the Institute for Divorce Financial Analysts, 22% of the divorces in the U.S. occur because of irreconcilable differences stemming from money issues. That is nearly ¼ of married couples who cannot remain together because of financial strain and stress.

Now of course I am not saying that taking control of your money and living debt-free is going to necessarily save your marriage, but just think about the influence that money has on a household and the frustration that can exist when there is additional pressure due to debt and a lack of money management. I am sure that you can see how eliminating this very stressful, very real issue can positively impact any relationship.

For many couples, discussions about their financial well-being is either off-limits or handled by one or the other in the relationship. I encourage you that if you are in a relationship, you must have open and honest conversations about spending habits, financial goals, and your shared vision for the future. When two people's ideals are not in alignment, it is a recipe for disaster, especially when one is a spender and one is not. The point is that as humans, it is common knowledge that we work better when we work together. When people are in agreement, they are better able to achieve positive results and make a greater impact.

Decisions about money and the direction that you want to point your finances should be a joint decision. In other words, if one person believes in stockpiling savings while the other wants to pay down debt, you will have a problem. If one wants to enjoy life today without any regard for tomorrow, you will have a problem. If one of you wants to only use credit cards while the other pays in cash, you will have a problem. No matter what your previous viewpoints or philosophies about money were, you must start fresh and get on the same page. I highly recommend that if any of this describes the financial discussions in your house that you pass on this book to your spouse or significant other so that they too can learn the tricks and tips that I have shared. It may be better for them to read it for themselves than to rely on the information being passed on secondhand.

Ultimately, you will need to be on the same page for you to make progress toward becoming debt-free and, more importantly, maintaining a lifestyle in which you dictate to your money as to what you want it to do. As I am sure you know, debt can easily creep back in if you stray from the plan or revert back to your previous bad habits and way of life. You are in this together and you must commit to being in it for the long-haul. Although I can't (and won't) guarantee that the advice provided here will salvage any bad relationship, at least you can alleviate the financial strain that causes couples so many challenges.

FOR INDIVIDUALS

Just because you do not have a partner to blame or to align with in your financial journey to debt-free living does not change the process at all. In fact, it is more important for you to be in agreement with yourself than if you were in a relationship. In this case, you have no one to blame for your debt burden other than yourself--but remember that we are not in the blame game here. My point is that as a single person, you only have yourself to be accountable to and to keep yourself on track. As difficult as financial situations and discussions can be, having positive self-talk with yourself is critical to your success in living the life that you want.

We all can be our own worst critics. From the limiting beliefs that have held us back to the lies that we tell ourselves, many people are their own worst enemy. Only you can determine your relationship with money; only you can change your perspective on your financial situation; only you can decide to make a change that will redirect the trajectory of your life. You can continue down the road that you have been traveling, stressed about your financial health, weighed down under a mountain of debt, and living paycheck to paycheck. On the other hand, you have the power to choose to live this way or not. You can decide that you are fed up with your current situation and you want more. You can choose to reduce your spending and limit your nonessential purchases. You can opt to unburden yourself from the debt and live a life that you have envisioned but never thought possible.

Do you see the pattern here? YOU have power if you have the desire and motivation to take back control, to manage what your money does, and to enjoy debt-free living. But you have to decide.

This book and my insights are simply that: insights into HOW to understand credit, examples of HOW to evaluate your financial health and HOW to develop a master plan for success. I have described what has worked for me and hopefully given you a clear path as to how you can do it too. What I cannot provide you with is the motivation to take that next step. That part is on you, but I want to encourage you that you are not alone. There are millions of people out there who are in your position now or who have been and are there to encourage you to keep pushing forward. People just like you and me who never saw the light at the end of the tunnel yet who have persevered, sacrificed, and overcome.

Many people are unwilling to share their personal financial struggles with others in fear of judgement or even pity. There is nothing to be ashamed of or embarrassed by when it comes to debt. Unless you were born with a silver spoon in your mouth or have never taken advantage of the extension of credit of any kind, most people can relate to the idea of debt at some level. As we talked about early, millions of people in the United States are in a debt situation of some kind and are more than likely stressed by their positions. So, again, you are not alone!

I also want to remind you that you did not get into this position overnight. It may have taken years of overspending, even decades of financial mismanagement to get you where you are today. You cannot possibly think that you are going to escape from underneath a mountain of debt overnight or even within the short-term. No. What we have been talking about is not a quick-fix or a get-rich-quick scheme. It will require dedication, consistency, and commitment.

You may be thinking, "I don't want to wait! I want to live a debt-free life now!" Well, I am sorry to tell you, my friend, that that may not be possible. Of course, depending upon your debt and your diligence with the plan, you may be in a better position than many and could possibly enjoy debt-free living within several months or years. But, again, it is up to you. I do not have any magic wand or fool-proof prescription that says "take this pill three times per day and POOF! You will be debt-free in three months!"

I am sorry to say that no such thing exists unless, of course, you hit the lottery. According to Lottery USA, "the odds of winning the Mega Millions jackpot are 1 in 302.6 million and the odds of winning the Powerball jackpot are 1 in 292.2 million. Combine those two and the odds of winning both jackpots for more than a billion dollars comes out to 1 in 88 quadrillion." If you have been secretly hoping that winning the lottery would be your ticket out from under your financial woes, I am sorry to burst your bubble.

Instead, you will have to put in the effort. You will have to dedicate yourself to developing and sticking to your master plan. You must consistently work toward the end goal in mind and if you do this, I CAN guarantee that you will reap the benefits and rewards of debt-free living. Just knowing that this is a possibility should bring a smile to your face.

MOTIVATE YOURSELF

If you are like most people, you might slip once in a while. Sticking to a budget is no different than sticking to a diet or exercise regimen. There are those who find these types of challenges easy and they quickly and easily adapt their routines to match their goals and objectives. There are others though who find it more difficult to create habits, for whom change is difficult, and motivation is not their strong suit. No matter in which category you fall, or somewhere in between, I believe that the power to persevere begins in the mind and that only you have control of it.

It does not matter what your tendencies or habits were previously. The past is the past and it is time to move forward. You are in control, and only you can drive change. Now I am not saying that it will be easy or that you won't make mistakes. I know that by making mistakes we learn and grow. Your budget will not be perfect the first time around and it may require major or minor changes along the way. As you become more comfortable with your master plan and develop new, more cost-effective spending habits, you will make adjustments and maybe some errors in judgment. But it is what you learn from these that will determine your success in achieving your ultimate goal. What have you learned from your spending habits in your 20's that you can apply to your lifestyle in your 30s? Where do you want them to be in your 40's?

While the journey may not be easy and it will certainly have its pitfalls and challenges, you will overcome them and stay on the path. I believe that you can do it but more importantly, you must believe that you can do it. Like anything in life that is challenging or difficult, you have to get back up and keep at it if you want to succeed.

I have put together a few ways that you can stay motivated and stay on track toward crushing your debt. I have used many of these strategies myself and I hope that you will find them helpful as well.

- **Set realistic goals.** There is no better way to crush

your dreams than to set goals that are unachievable and frankly, unrealistic. You would not set a goal of losing 20 lbs. in one month so why would you set a lofty and unattainable short-term goal for your debt plan? If you have $50k in debt, you cannot expect to crush it in 24 months on a salary of $40k. Remember that although being aggressive toward your debt is good, you still have to eat and live somewhere. You are setting yourself up for disappointment and to more easily derail your motivation when your goals are not realistic.

- **Public accountability.** As I mentioned earlier, if you are in a relationship, discussing your plans and vision with your partner is critical to crushing your debt and sticking to the plan. Whether you are single or in a relationship, public accountability motivates us to stick to the plan. No one wants to be called out for not following through. Share your vision and goals with friends and family and keep them updated as to your progress. Remember that there is no shame in the game and by sharing with others, you may actually get some budgeting tips from others who have or are going through the same process.

- **Vision board.** In many self-help and self-improvement circles, this idea of creating a vision board is encouraged to help people to see where they want to go. Isn't your goal of living a debt-free life a vision of how you want to see your life in the future? Create a vision board to help motivate you and keep you on track. Every time that you are tempted to veer astray from your master plan, look at your vision board to keep you focused. The prospect of a bright future hopefully is more powerful than the instant gratification that you might receive today.

- **Treat yourself.** Again, back to my example of trying to follow a strict diet. Most dieters fall off the wagon and overindulge if they feel that the eating plan is too restrictive or strict. They may go out and binge on junk food at the first chance they get to combat the feelings of being caged in. The same holds true for your budget and master plan to pay off debt. If you limit yourself to the extreme, not allowing any minor occasional indulgences, you may become irritated by the constant limitations. Some people may even feel resentment toward their significant other if they feel as if they cannot live. To avoid these feelings, treat yourself once in a while. If you recall, our master plan did include 10% for rewarding yourself for sticking to the plan.

- **Track your success.** Early on I used the phrase, "eat the elephant one bite at a time." I was referring to the process of tackling your debt in small increments or one bite at a time. In other words, set small, reasonable goals within your overall goal and keep track of your progress. Each milestone is something to celebrate. Now I am not talking about throwing a big, expensive party when you have paid off $5000 in debt but you could treat yourself to a nice dinner out. But you will not know when you achieved your goals or reached certain milestones if you do not track your progress. Your master plan will include not only the first three months' evaluation of your finances and spending but monthly checkups to ensure that you are staying on track to crush your debt.

It is now game time. It's time to implement and stick to your plan. The longer that you put it off, the more debt will accrue, and the more stress will weigh down on you. There is no better time than NOW to get started. Push away those thoughts of how you got into this position and the regrets over decisions gone wrong. It is time to take control of your life and your money and take one step closer to living debt-free.

SUMMARY - IT'S GAME TIME!: STICK TO THE PLAN

- If you are in a relationship, open and honest discussions are necessary to move forward with a debt pay-off plan. Both parties must be in agreement with the plan as well as committed to its success.

- Individuals must rely on the power within to motivate themselves and stay on track toward living debt-free.
- Crushing your debt is going to require diligence, consistency, and will-power but with the right motivation, you can be well on your way to debt-free living.

In the beginning I told you that I was buried under more than $100k worth of debt and I was able to pay it off within five years. I would be lying if I told you that it was easy or that I didn't want to give up occasionally (or maybe often). But the feeling that I had when I made the final payment was something that I had never experienced before. It was a combination of pride, accomplishment, and in fact, I shed tears of joy. I know that I had sacrificed over those five years, but I had done something that many people think is impossible. I paid down more than $100k in debt and was now living debt-free. Can you feel it? The roar of the crowd? The smiles all around.

There is no better feeling than working hard for something and reaping the fruits of your labor. Although I had been nervous, frustrated and stressed before I began my debt pay off plan, I was so excited for what life would be like after that I was not going to let anything stop me. You may be wondering how I was able to remain debt free. I felt so empowered by this experience and accomplishing such a feat that I just knew that I never again wanted to feel the stress of financial challenges. I had changed my perspective and habits along the way and there was nothing in the world that could entice me to go back.

As much as I would like to believe it, my story is not that out of the ordinary. Although the amount I owed was high, don't forget that it took me five years to finally pay it off. That is 60 months of budgeting, carefully monitoring my spending, and diligently using my envelope system. There were many battles inside my brain and struggles to stay on track. But the most important thing is that I did it. Whether it took me five years or ten years, I was determined to continue with my master plan and to eventually live debt-free.

There are many others who have accomplished this amazing feat as well. Even though the number of people burdened by debt is unsurprisingly large, there are also millions of others who have overcome the stress of debt and are living the life that they want. Which group do you want to be in?

I chose to follow the route of living debt-free and I hope that you will too.

CONCLUSION

If you remember, I was in your shoes. I was drowning in debt, stressed, frustrated, and could not foresee a future in which I did not have any debt. Until I got sick and tired of being sick and tired!

I decided to take the bull by the horns and do something about my debt. I no longer wanted to live paycheck to paycheck having my money disappear each month. In other words, I decided to take control.

I hope that throughout this book I have offered you useful tools to help you to understand how your mindset plays a role in your financial situation; strategies to evaluate and monitor your spending; proven method of paying for nonessentials, and provided you with the motivation to not only get started but to continue on this path toward debt-free living.

It was my intention to demonstrate that debt-free living is not a pipe dream or only something that the truly wealthy enjoy. No. Debt-free living is a very real possibility if you are willing to put in the effort, to be patient, and to stick with your plan.

I believe in you and now you must believe in yourself. Now that you have a better grasp on what debt is and how it negatively impacts your life, I hope that you too will dream bigger and have a vision for your future that includes debt-free living.

Now go out there and crush that debt and get started living the life that you want.

If you found the material in this book to be useful and enjoyed reading it, please be sure to write a review on Amazon so that others may benefit from its life-changing advice.

As a person formerly in your shoes, I want to welcome you to this lifestyle of debt-free living and encourage you to keep pushing forward no matter the obstacles, challenges or feelings that get in the way. You will thank me for it later and I hope that you will consider paying it forward by sharing your success story with someone else to inspire them to crush their debt and begin living debt-free like you did.

REFERENCES

1. DEBT: WHAT IS IT, REALLY?

1. https://www.debt.org/faqs/americans-in-debt/#:~:text=Consider%
   20these%20statistics%20about%20personal%20debt%20in%20America%20%
   3A&text=Total%20U.S.%20consumer%20debt%20is%20at%20%
   2413.86%20trillion.
2. https://www.nitrocollege.com/research/average-student-loan-debt